DESIGN
AND
APPLICATION
OF
LINEAR
COMPUTATIONAL
CIRCUITS

DESIGN
AND
APPLICATION
OF
LINEAR
COMPUTATIONAL
CIRCUITS

GEORGE L. BATTEN, JR.

TAB Professional and Reference Books

Division of TAB BOOKS Inc.
P.O. Box 40, Blue Ridge Summit, PA 17214

FIRST EDITION

FIRST PRINTING

Library of Congress Cataloging in Publication Data

Batten Jr., George L.
    Design and application of linear computational
    circuits.

    Bibliography: p.
    Includes index.
    1. Operational amplifiers. 2. Electronic analog
computers—Circuits. I. Title.
TK7871.58.06B39   1987   621.3815′35   86-5952
ISBN 0-8306-2727-8

Contents

Introduction

A NALOG COMPUTATIONAL CIRCUITS ARE QUITE USEFUL IN A variety of applications. Due to advances in integrated circuit technology, they are inexpensive to build. This book is a guide to the design, construction, and use of analog computational circuits.

Chapter 1 is an introduction to the subject. Some of the uses of analog computational circuits are listed. Because the integrated circuit operational amplifier (op amp) forms the heart of these circuits, a review of the op amp is given. Finally, hints on the construction of the circuits are discussed.

Two power supplies are needed to power the circuits in this book. Chapter 2 covers the construction of both the bipolar regulated supply for the op amps and the regulated supply for the relays. The relay power supply is a + 5 Vdc supply, which makes it useful for logic circuit work.

In computation, accurate voltages are needed. Chapter 3 shows how to obtain reference voltages and covers the general area of multiplication by constant coefficients.

Chapters 4 through 7 present the analyses of computational circuits. Addition and subtraction are covered in Chapter 4. Chapter 5 examines multiplication and division of variables and obtaining squares and square roots. Integration and differentiation are presented in Chapter 6. Function generation, particularly log-antilog and sine-cosine, is examined in Chapter 7.

Programming the circuits to solve differential equations, and to generate other functions, is discussed in Chapter 8. Chapter 9 presents elementary process control applications of the circuits.

The bibliography at the end of the text is not meant to be exhaustive. It does present several books which are extremely useful and very readable.

Chapter 1

Introduction to
Analog Computers

A COMPUTER IS A DEVICE (OR COMBINATION OF DEVICES) THAT performs mathematical calculations. It may be a mechanical device (such as the abacus or slide rule) or an electronic device. The very first electronic computers were *analog* computers, which were so named because the variables representing physical quantities were simulated with analogous voltages. Analog computers are composed of circuits that perform specific mathematical operations, such as addition, subtraction, multiplication, division, integration and function generation. The computer is programmed (i.e., set up to solve a particular equation) by connecting the various circuits in the proper sequence. Inputs to the circuits are voltages that vary with time in a prescribed manner. The output voltage is the solution to the equation.

As computer technology advanced, the electronic analog computer (EAC) gradually yielded ground to the *digital* computer. The digital computer is simply a counting machine, handling individual digits at high speeds. Its basic mathematical operations are addition, subtraction, multiplication and division. Algorithms have allowed the digital computer to expand its function generation capacity, and clever programming allows a broad range of calculus to be performed. In addition, the

1

digital computer's memory makes it an extremely versatile device. As a result, the digital computer has displaced the electronic analog computer as king of the computing machines.

In spite of the digital computer's supremacy, the EAC has carved out a niche of applications in which it is the computer of choice. The EAC is most useful in solving differential equations, especially non-linear differential equations and systems of equations. Of course, the digital computer can be used to approximate solutions to differential equations, but often times the programming involved is complex or the solution requires much CPU (central processing unit) time. This is particularly true of non-linear differential equations. Programming the EAC, however, is relatively simple. The appropriate computational circuits are connected by patch cords, the initial conditions are set, and the output voltage as a function of time is read off of a meter, oscilloscope, or strip chart recorder. With the EAC, one does not need to be a mathematician in order to solve a host of difficult equations.

Although the EAC is unsurpassed in solving differential equations, its most important use is in the area of simulation and process control. In performing real-time algebraic and dynamic computations, the EAC can be used to monitor and control processes. The reference voltage source (Chapter 3) provides standard voltages for computing and, in conjunction with the constant coefficient multipliers described in that chapter, provides set points, test signals and constant inputs for controllers. The adder/subtractor module described in Chapter 4 adds and/or subtracts signals. Since the input gains can be adjusted individually, the input voltages can be converted to process units (pounds, gallons, degrees centigrade, etc.). The multiplication/division/square/square root module of Chapter 5 is extremely flexible, and when provided with appropriate input sensors, it can display computed values, such as flow rate. The integrator (Chapter 6) is often used in industrial applications to generate a time-varying set point that is then fed into a process controller. The addition of one resistor to the integrator allows the simulation of time lags in a process. The function generators in Chapter 7 are more often used in computation, but are sometimes useful in industrial applications as signal generators.

The circuits in this book are thus useful to the

mathematician or the process control engineer; however, one does not need to be an electrical engineer in order to build and use them. Nor does one need to be rich in order to afford them. Thanks to advances in integrated circuit technology, a general-purpose IC operational amplifier (which forms the heart of most of the circuits in this book) can be purchased for less than a dollar. And since the computational characteristics of the operational amplifier are determined primarily by the feedback network surrounding it, an in-depth knowledge of the operational amplifier is not necessary.

The next section will present a general overview of the operational amplifier. The reader who is interested in further study will find several good references listed in the bibliography.

THE OPERATIONAL AMPLIFIER

Almost all of the analog computational circuits described in this book employ the operational amplifier, or op amp for short. The op amp is a direct-coupled high-gain amplifier with differential inputs. Feedback is used to control its performance characteristics. The *ideal* operational amplifier has certain properties: infinite open-loop (i.e., no feedback) gain, infinite input impedance, zero output impedance, infinite bandwidth, and zero input offset voltage. Although the ideal op amp does not exist, these ideal characteristics are closely approximated by the modern, inexpensive IC op amp.

The op amp is represented by the symbol shown in Fig. 1-1. The op amp has two input terminals and one output terminal. If a positive voltage is applied to the noninverting (+) input, the op amp output e_o will be a positive voltage. If a positive voltage is applied to the inverting (–) input, the output e_o will be negative.

The power supply for the op amp is a bipolar supply; i.e., there are two voltages of equal magnitude but opposite polarity with respect to common. The supply voltages (V + , V –) are shown in Fig. 1-1; however, they are usually omitted on most schematics. Typical supply voltages range from ± 9 V to ± 18 V. The supply voltages should be ± 2 V larger than the maximum output voltage, and input voltages should be less than supply voltages.

As stated previously, an ideal op amp has certain characteristics which are only approximated by real op

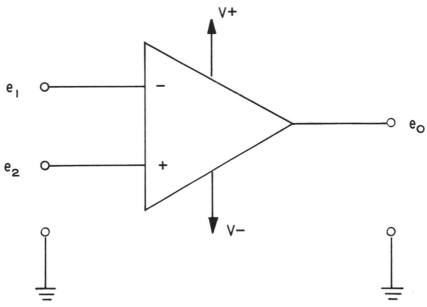

Fig. 1-1. Schematic symbol for the op amp.

amps. Let us consider how well the 741 op amp com-
pares with the ideal. The 741 is an inexpensive, popular frequency-compensated general-purpose op amp that
is used frequently throughout this book.

The output voltage e_o of an op amp with no feedback (i.e., open-loop operation) is $A_{vo}e_i$, where A_{vo} is
the open-loop voltage gain and e_i is the input voltage.
For an ideal op amp, A_{vo} is infinite. The 741 lists an
open-loop gain of 200,000. Although this is not infinite,
it is very, very high. More expensive op amps can be
purchased which give gains of more than 1,000,000.

The infinite input impedance of an ideal op amp
means that the op amp input serves as neither a source
nor sink for current. The 741 lists an input impedance
of 2,000,000 ohms; again, not infinite, but extremely
high. FET-input op amps are capable of providing input impedances of more than 10^{12} ohms.

The zero output impedance of the ideal op amp is,
of course, not achievable in reality. Real op amps do,
however, have very low output impedances (usually less
than 100 ohms). The 741 lists an output impedance of
75 ohms.

The infinite bandwidth of the ideal op amp means

that the open-loop voltage gain remains constant as frequency is varied. In reality, the gain of a nonideal op amp remains fairly constant over a small range (less than 10 Hz) and drops off rapidly after that. The 741 lists a bandwidth of 1 MHz; however, it can provide substantial gains only up to approximately 10 kHz.

Since the op amp is a differential input amplifier, the output voltage e_o will be zero if $e_1 = e_2$ in an ideal op amp. This is what is meant by a zero input offset voltage. In actual practice, we find that e_o is on the order of 1-2 mV for the 741 when $e_1 = e_2$. Precision op amps have lower input offset voltages (0.05 - 0.1 mV). Some op amps (including the 741) have null terminals that allow the offset to be removed. The procedure for doing this with the 741 is shown in Fig. 1-2. When more than one op amp is included in a single package, the offset null terminals are usually not present. In general, small offset voltages will not adversely affect the performance of the circuits described in this book.

Although the properties of real op amps fall short of the ideal, the error associated with nonideality is small, usually less than 10%. We are thus safe in assuming that the op amps are ideal for design purposes. Consideration of these ideal characteristics leads to two rules

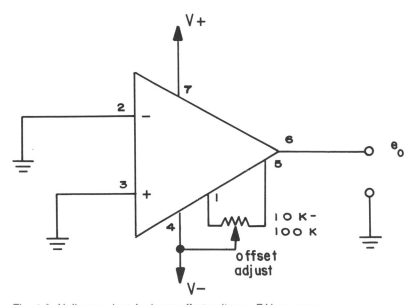

Fig. 1-2. Null procedure for input offset voltage—741 op amp.

for circuit analysis. Since an infinite gain would result in an infinite e_o if e_1 is not equal to e_2, rule 1 states that *we treat both inputs as if they are at the same potential*. And since there is an infinite input impedance, rule 2 states that *there is no current flow into either input terminal*. The use of these rules in the analysis of feedback networks around the op amp will be illustrated in the next section.

THE INVERTING AMPLIFIER

At this point we are familiar with the op amp. We know nothing of what is inside the op amp; we only know that the op amp is a differential input amplifier with certain ideal properties. The op amp's performance characteristics are determined by the feedback network surrounding the amp. This section will demonstrate an analysis of the feedback network in one of the most popular op amp configurations, the inverting amplifier.

The inverting amplifier is shown in Fig. 1-3. Note that power supply and offset adjustment connections are not shown. The input signal e_i is applied to the inverting input and the noninverting input is grounded. According to rule 1, since the noninverting input is at ground potential, the inverting input is at ground potential (point X). The currents at point X must sum to zero, so that $i_1 = -i_2$. Now the two currents are easily obtained by Ohm's law:

$$i_1 = \frac{e_i}{R_1} \qquad\qquad \textbf{(1-1)}$$

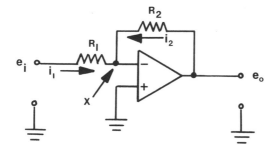

Fig. 1-3. The inverting amplifier.

and

$$i_2 = \frac{e_o}{R_2} \qquad \textbf{(1-2)}$$

Combining these two equations with the relationship $i_1 = -i_2$ yields the following equation:

$$e_o = \frac{-R_2 e_i}{R_1} \qquad \textbf{(1-3)}$$

In other words, the output voltage is determined solely by the input voltage and the two resistors R_1 and R_2. Equation (1-3) may be rewritten as

$$e_o = A_v e_i \qquad \textbf{(1-4)}$$

where A_v is the closed-loop gain and is equal, in this case, to $-R_2/R_1$.

The circuit of Fig. 1-3 will be used many times in the circuits that comprise this book. The inverting amplifier will be used to scale the variables (i.e., multiply by constant coefficients) and simply to change the sign of a variable or constant (by making R_1 equal to R_2).

According to equation (1-3), any values of R_1 and R_2 may be used to set the closed-loop gain of the amplifier, since it is the ratio of R_2 to R_1 that we are interested in. That is not entirely correct. Resistor R_1 sets the input impedance for the circuit, and this should be at least ten times the output impedance of the previous stage. Since the output impedance of op amps is on the order of 100 ohms, R_1 should be at least 1000 ohms.

For an ideal op amp, there are no restrictions on the value of R_2. For real op amps, however, restrictions occur. Our second design rule states that no current flows into either op amp terminal. That rule is not true for nonideal op amps. An input offset current will be found in nonideal op amps, and the voltage drop created by this current will be proportional to both R_1 and R_2. To minimize this error voltage, R_1 and R_2 should not be greater than 20,000 ohms. Resistors on the order of 10,000 ohms are suitable for most applications.

Equation (1-3) was derived assuming that the op

amp was ideal. What are the magnitudes of the errors arising from this assumption? Actually, the errors are quite small. If one allows for a finite gain, equation (1-3) is replaced by equation (1-5):

$$e_o = - \frac{A_{vo}R_2}{(1 + A_{vo}) R_1 + R_2} e_i \qquad \textbf{(1-5)}$$

In other words, the closed-loop gain of equation (1-3) is $A_v = - R_2/R_1$, while the closed-loop gain of equation (1-5) is $A_v = - A_{vo}R_2/(1 + A_{vo})R_1 + R_2$. Let's assume that we want a closed-loop gain of $- 2$, and we choose $R_2 = 20,000$ ohms and $R_1 = 10,000$ ohms. From equation (1-3) (which assumes ideal behavior), we have $A_v = - 2$. For a 741 op amp ($A_{vo} = 2 \times 10^5$), equation (1-5) yields $A_v = - 1.99997$. The error introduced by assuming an infinite open-loop gain is only 0.0015%! This is very good accuracy from an op amp that costs 79¢!

There are other corrections which can be made to equation (1-3), such as a correction for noninfinite input impedance. In general, these corrections are not necessary for our purposes. Readers who are interested in the nature of these corrections should consult the books listed in the bibliography.

The next section will present another example of feedback analysis of op amp circuits.

THE SUMMING AMPLIFIER

The summing amplifier is shown in Fig. 1-4. According to our first rule of circuit analysis, point X is at ground potential, so that $i_T = - i_4$. The total current i_T is just the sum of the currents through R_1, R_2 and R_3. Using Ohm's law to express the currents in terms of resistances and voltages yields equation (1-6).

$$\frac{e_1}{R_1} + \frac{e_2}{R_2} + \frac{e_3}{R_3} = - \frac{e_o}{R_4} \qquad \textbf{(1-6)}$$

Rearranging equation (1-6) gives the output voltage as a function of input voltages:

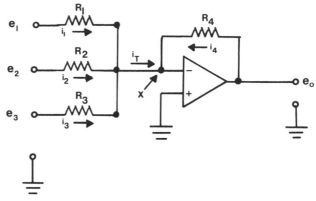

Fig. 1-4. The summing amplifier.

$$e_o = - R_4 \left(\frac{e_1}{R_1} + \frac{e_2}{R_2} + \frac{e_3}{R_3} \right) \qquad (1\text{-}7)$$

In other words, the output voltage is a scaled sum of input voltages, the scaling being performed by the resistors $R_1 - R_4$. If all resistors are of equal value, then the output is the negative of the sum without scaling.

This is the way the mathematical operation of addition is performed with op amps. As with the inverting amplifier, corrections for noninfinite gain, input impedance, etc., may be employed, but their contribution is usually small.

The types of feedback networks necessary to perform other mathematical operations, such as multiplication and division of variables, integration, etc., will be examined in subsequent chapters. The approach is always the same: the feedback network determines the type of operation that is performed.

CONSTRUCTION HINTS

The purpose of constructing these analog computational circuits is to obtain relatively inexpensive, efficient and flexible circuits for use in process control and/or computation. Where possible, commercially available ICs or modules will be used instead of discrete circuits. The costs of these modules and ICs are not prohibitive; however, if cost is an overriding concern, the books listed in the bibliography can be consulted for alternative circuit designs.

If these circuits are to be used in a production environment, each circuit should be enclosed in a plastic or metal box. They can then be used as control modules. Every effort has been made to ensure that each module is designed with maximum flexibility of use in mind. If these circuits are intended for use in a laboratory environment, they may be assembled on a universal breadboard socket as needed.

The 741 op amp is used frequently in the circuits which comprise this book. The 741 is a very stable device. If other op amps are used, it may be necessary to bypass the power supply lines to the op amp to improve circuit stability. This is shown in Fig. 1-5.

There are three considerations which deserve special mention. First, it is absolutely vital that the polarity of the op amp is maintained. A carefully designed circuit will be ruined if the polarity of the power supply is reversed at the op amp. Second, when mounting components on circuit boards, be sure to use a low-wattage soldering iron. Excessive temperatures can damage an op amp as it can any other semiconductor. Third, do not exceed the maximum input or output voltages

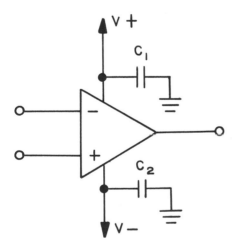

$C_1, C_2 = 0.1\,\mu F$ ceramic

or

$1.0\,\mu F$ tantalum

Fig. 1-5. Op-amp stabilization.

of the op amp. Since we will be using a $\pm$ 15 Vdc power supply, be sure to restrict input and output voltages to no more than $\pm$ 10 Vdc.

The reader is advised to read each chapter carefully before beginning construction. It is also a good idea to breadboard each circuit before permanently mounting the components on a printed circuit.

Where possible, components have been used that are readily available to the general public (such as Radio Shack components). For those components not available at Radio Shack, addresses of suppliers have been listed.

Chapter 2

Power Supplies

T WO POWER SUPPLIES ARE NEEDED TO POWER THE CIR-
cuits described in the following chapters. The circuits themselves use a bipolar (± 15 Vdc) regulated supply. The relays necessary to reset the integrators and turn
on the quadrature require a separate supply. In this chapter we examine the design and construction of both
power supplies.

DUAL-POLARITY REGULATED POWER SUPPLY

The op amps, specialized ICs and modules in the
following circuits require a bipolar power supply; i.e.,
the supply must deliver a positive and negative voltage
of equal magnitude with respect to circuit ground. This
is easily achieved with the circuit shown in Fig. 2-1.

The operation of the circuit is as follows. By ground-
ing the center tap on the transformer, the diode bridge
D1 - D4 becomes two full-wave center-tapped rectifier
circuits. The output at the junction of D3 and D4 is positive with respect to ground, while the output at the junction of D1 and D2 is negative with respect to ground.
These output voltages are filtered (C1 and C2—note the
reversal in polarity), regulated (IC1, IC2), and bypassed.

The ICs in Fig. 2-1 belong to a class of chips known

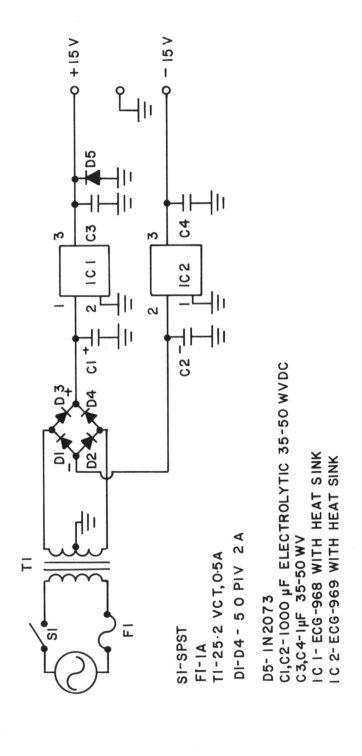

SI-SPST
FI-IA
TI-25·2 VCT, 0·5A
DI-D4 - 50 PIV 2A

D5- IN 2073
CI,C2-1000 μF ELECTROLYTIC 35-50 WVDC
C3,C4-IμF 35-50WV
IC I- ECG-968 WITH HEAT SINK
IC 2 ECG-969 WITH HEAT SINK

Fig. 2-1. Dual-polarity regulated power supply.

as *three-terminal voltage regulators*. These are fixed-voltage monolithic IC regulators that require no external components and are essentially blow-out proof. With proper heatsinks, they can deliver more than 1 amp. Almost any of the available three-terminal regulators can be used. The ones shown in Fig. 2-1 are Sylvania devices and can be obtained from Philips ECG, Inc., P.O. Box 3277, 1025 Westminster Drive, Williamsport, PA 17701.

Diode D5 is a clamp diode on the positive output and is used to prevent a problem known as *latch-up*. Latch-up is an overload phenomenon that can occur in feedback amplifiers and usually results in the amplifier resting at one extreme of full output voltage. The problem can be corrected by turning off the power to the amp or regulator and starting over again, but this is inconvenient. The diode clamp ensures that the output retains polarity while losing gain in overload, thus preventing latch-up.

The circuit of Fig. 2-1 can be fabricated on a piece of perf board and mounted in an experimenter's box. Circuit layout is shown in Fig. 2-2. Bridge diodes D1 - D4 may be purchased as a single unit from Radio Shack or other suppliers. A top view of the placement of the board and other components in an experimenter's box is shown in Fig. 2-3. If the box does not allow for vertical placement of the perf board, a horizontal placement may be used as shown in Fig. 2-4.

A frontal view of the power supply is shown in Fig. 2-5. The choice of output jacks should be based on convenience. Banana jacks, terminal strips, or barrier terminals may be used.

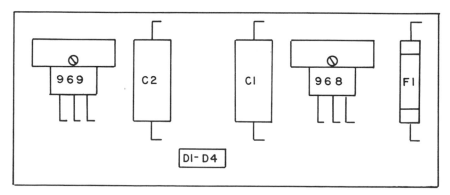

Fig. 2-2. Circuit layout for Fig. 2-1.

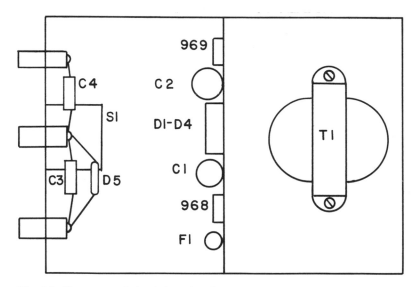

Fig. 2-3. Placement of circuit board and components.

RELAY POWER SUPPLY

The relay supply voltage will depend upon the choice of relays. Because of the availability of mini SPDT relays with +5 Vdc coils, the author chose to build a +5 Vdc relay power supply. This supply can also be used with logic circuits which require +5 Vdc.

The circuit is shown in Fig. 2-6. In this application, diodes D1 - D4 form a bridge that delivers a positive voltage at the junction of D3 and D4. The output is filtered by C1, regulated by IC1 and bypassed by C2. The three-terminal regulator used is a μA7805 5-Vdc positive regu-

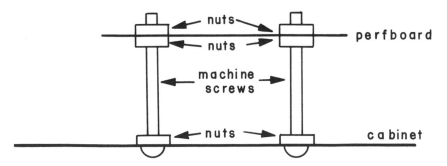

Fig. 2-4. Horizontal placement of perf board.

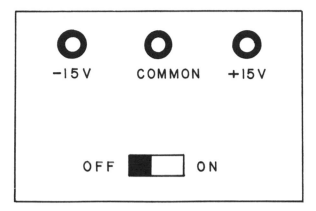

Fig. 2-5. Front view of power supply.

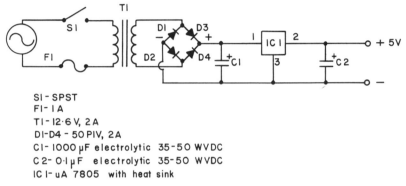

S1 - SPST
F1 - 1 A
T1 - 12·6 V, 2 A
D1-D4 - 50 PIV, 2 A
C1 - 1000 µF electrolytic 35-50 WVDC
C2 - 0·1 µF electrolytic 35-50 WVDC
IC 1 - uA 7805 with heat sink

Fig. 2-6. Relay power supply.

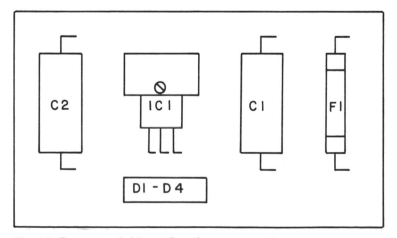

Fig. 2-7. Recommended layout for relay power supply.

17

lator and is available at Radio Shack. Any three-terminal 5-V regulator will do, however. The regulator should be equipped with a heatsink.

As with the bipolar supply, the circuit can be fabricated on perf board. Recommended layout is given in Fig. 2-7.

Chapter 3

Reference Voltages

$\mathbf{A}$ CCURATE REFERENCE VOLTAGES ARE NEEDED FOR COMPU-
tation. This chapter describes the construction of
a reference voltage source which supplies two positive
and two negative reference voltages. Two methods of
performing multiplication by constant coefficients will
also be examined so that the reference voltages may be
scaled up or down.

REFERENCE VOLTAGE SOURCE

A suitable reference voltage source is shown in Fig.
3-1. The first thing to notice about the circuit is that it
uses a single-ended supply. This ensures that the circuit will start properly. If a bipolar supply is used, the
circuit may not start.

The circuit contains two feedback loops: a positive
loop through R1 and a negative loop through R3. Initially, the output of the op amp is fed through R1 to the
noninverting input. When the voltage across the zener
diode D1 reaches the breakdown voltage, the noninverting input is fixed at the zener voltage. This gives reference voltage e_{o1}. Since in closed-loop operation the
potentials at both inputs to the op amp are equal, the
negative feedback network of R2-R3 simply scales the
voltage e_{o1} to a different level (e_{o2}). The relationship is

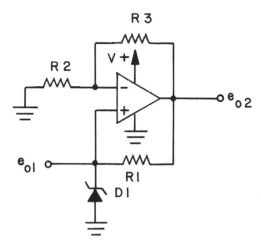

Fig. 3-1. Reference voltage source.

given by equation (3-1):

$$e_{o2} = e_{o1} \frac{(R_2 + R_3)}{R_2} \tag{3-1}$$

The circuit of Fig. 3-2 is a more useful reference source and is the one that will be used later for computational purposes. All three amplifiers are 741 op amps. The circuit of A1 is just the voltage source shown in Fig. 3-1, except that R2 in Fig. 3-1 has been replaced with a potentiometer. Adjustment of the potentiometer (using two or three different digital voltmeters at the output of A1) allows the + 10.00 V output to be set precisely. The circuits of A2 and A3 are just inverting amplifiers such as the one shown in Fig. 1-3. Since R4 = R5 and R6 = R7, the gain is unity and the outputs are just the negatives of the inputs. Potentiometers R8 and R9 are used for offset null adjustment.

The reference voltage circuit is easily fabricated on a preprinted PC universal IC board (Radio Shack 276-168). Suggested component layout is shown in Fig. 3-3.

The circuit board should be mounted in an experimenter's box or cabinet. The author used a 4-terminal strip for outputs, as shown in Fig. 3-4A. Pushbutton terminals, barrier strips, or banana jacks could also be used. A three-position dual-row barrier strip was used in the

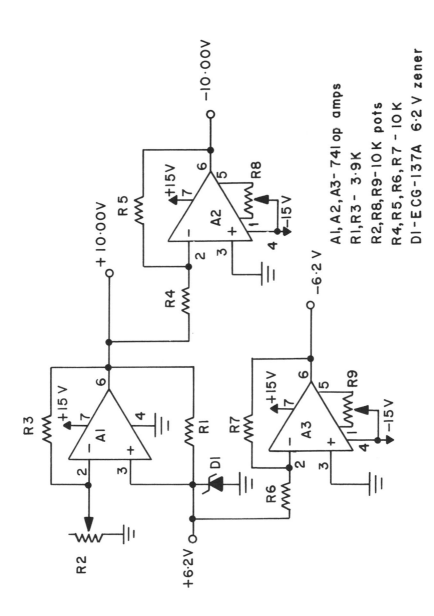

Fig. 3-2. Practical reference voltage source.

21

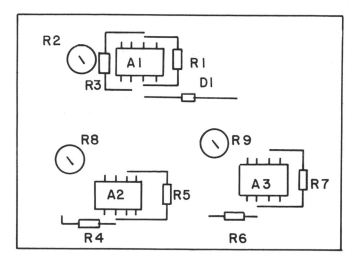

Fig. 3-3. Component layout for the reference voltage source.

rear of the cabinet for power supply connections, as shown in Fig. 3-4B.

MULTIPLICATION BY CONSTANT COEFFICIENTS: INVERTING AMPLIFIER

Multiplication by constant coefficients and sign in-

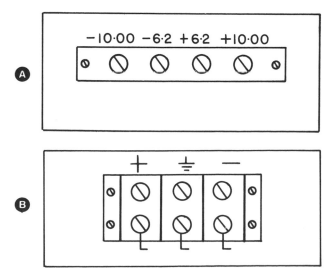

Fig. 3-4. (A) Front view of reference voltage source (B) rear view.

version are the two operations most frequently performed with analog computational circuits. These operations are easily accomplished with the inverting amplifier of Fig. 1-3. A flexible circuit for both multiplication *and* sign inversion is shown in Fig. 3-5.

The IC used in Fig. 3-5 is a dual operational amplifier; i.e., there are two separate op amps included in a single, 8-pin DIP package. This chip offers two 741-type op amps in the space of one. Since there are only 8 pins, there are no offset null pins for either op amp. Offset voltages for this IC are small, however, and can usually be ignored. Both op amps share common power supply pins.

The second amp simply inverts the voltage supplied to it, since R1 = R2. The first amp is adjusted so that the constant coefficient can be set. At the output of the first amp, $-e_o$, the relationship to input voltage is

$$-e_o = \frac{-\text{Gain}\, e_i}{R} \qquad (3\text{-}2)$$

At the output of the second amp, e_o, we have

$$e_o = \frac{\text{Gain}}{R}\, e_i \qquad (3\text{-}3)$$

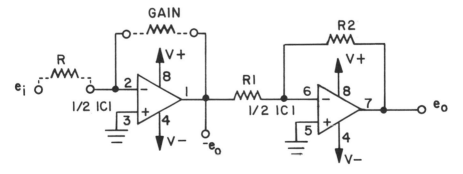

ICI- 1458 DUAL OP AMP (RADIO SHACK 276-038)

R - INPUT RESISTOR (IK ⩽ R ⩽ 20K)

GAIN-GAIN RESISTOR (IK ⩽ R ⩽ 20K)

RI, R2- 10K

Fig. 3-5. Multiplication by constant coefficient and sign inversion.

The resistors used in this circuit, as well as the rest of the circuits in this book, should be precision resistors and should observe the limitations on values described in Chapter 1.

For laboratory applications, the circuit of Fig. 3-5 may be constructed with IC breadboard sockets (Radio Shack 276-169, 276-174, 276-175) as needed. For use in industrial environments, the circuits should be fabricated on a universal IC board and enclosed in a plastic or metal box. Component layout for such a circuit, containing two constant coefficient multipliers, is shown in Fig. 3-6. External connections are shown in Fig. 3-7A and 3-7B. As with the reference voltage source, power supply connections are at the rear of the cabinet, and inputs, outputs and resistances are connected at the front of the cabinet with terminal strips.

MULTIPLICATION BY
CONSTANT COEFFICIENTS: POTENTIOMETERS

The multiplication method described in the previous section allows for gains greater than, less than, or equal to one. The method described in this section al-

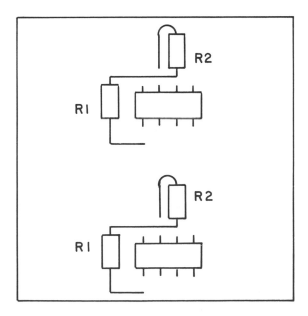

Fig. 3-6. Component layout for constant coefficient multiplier.

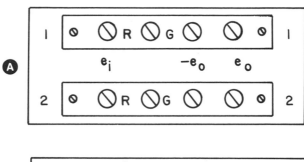

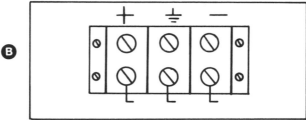

Fig. 3-7. (A) Front view of constant coefficient multiplier (B) rear view.

lows for gains less than or equal to one, and does not permit sign inversion. Nevertheless, the simplicity of this method makes it extremely useful. This method will be used almost exclusively for setting initial conditions and other reference voltages (in conjunction with the reference voltage source).

The principle behind the coefficient-setting potentiometer is shown in Fig. 3-8. A potential is applied to one end of the potentiometer, with the other end grounded. The voltage at the wiper is then continuously variable between 0 volts and the value applied to the high end. If the + 10.00-volt terminal of the reference supply is used, the coefficient-setting potentiometer can provide any initial condition or fixed voltage needed for calculation.

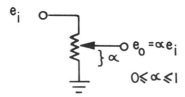

Fig. 3-8. The coefficient-setting potentiometer.

A practical circuit involving the potentiometer is shown in Fig. 3-9. The op amp is operated in the *voltage follower* configuration. In this configuration, there is 100% feedback through the inverting input. This results in the output equalling the input to the noninverting terminal. The gain is thus unity, but the input impedance of the circuit is now the input impedance of the op amp, which is extremely high. The voltage follower does not load the potentiometer, because of its near-infinite input impedance.

Two types of potentiometers are recommended. The ten-turn precision potentiometer is easy to mount in a box, and can be fitted with a circular concentric numbered dial (Amphenol 730-1350). Its resistance tolerance is ± 3%, and its linearity tolerance is ± 0.1%. It can be ordered from Amphenol Sales Division, 2875 South 25th Avenue, Broadview, Illinois 60153 (312/345-4260).

The fifteen-turn rectangular potentiometer is convenient for breadboarding and is considerably less expensive than the ten-turn type. It does not readily allow for mounting in a box and does not use a numbered dial. Its mechanical life is also somewhat limited (200 turns). The two main attractions of this type of potentiometer are low cost and ease in breadboarding. They can be pur-

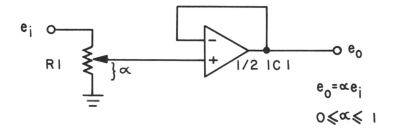

$$e_o = \alpha e_i$$
$$0 \leqslant \alpha \leqslant 1$$

RI-IOK TEN-TURN PRECISION POT

(AMPHENOL 205-103)

or

IOK FIFTEEN-TURN CERMET POT

(DIGI-KEY 0IBI4)

ICI- 1458 DUAL OP AMP

Fig. 3-9. Practical coefficient-setting potentiometer circuit.

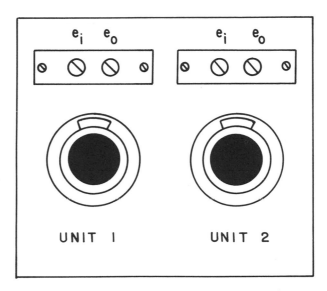

Fig. 3-10. Front view of coefficient-setting potentiometer.

chased from Digi-Key Corporation, Highway 32 South, P.O. Box 677, Thief River Falls, MN 56701.

Since a dual operational amplifier is used in Fig. 3-9, two ten-turn potentiometers may be conveniently mounted in a single box, which is shown in Fig. 3-10. Again, power supply connections are at the back of the cabinet.

Chapter 4

Addition and Subtraction

THE METHOD BY WHICH ADDITION IS PERFORMED USING OP-
erational amplifiers was studied in Chapter 1. A
brief review is given here. The summing amplifier (Fig.
4-1) has one feedback resistor (R_4) and any number of
input resistors (in this case, three). Since the op amp
is assumed to be ideal, no current is drawn and point
X is at ground potential, thus $i_T = -i_4$. The total current i_T is the sum of the three currents i_1, i_2, i_3. From
Ohm's law, we arrive at the expression for output
voltage:

$$e_o = -R_4 \left(\frac{e_1}{R_1} + \frac{e_2}{R_2} + \frac{e_3}{R_3} \right) \qquad \textbf{(4-1)}$$

This is the basic equation for addition with op amps.

Subtraction is just the inverse of addition, so it could
be accomplished by inverting the sign of the particular
input voltage to be subtracted (with an inverting amplifier) prior to the input of the circuit of Fig. 4-1. An easier method is available, however, and is shown in Fig.
4-2. The number of inputs have been limited to provide
for mathematical tractability.

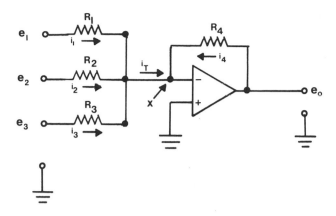

Fig. 4-1. The summing amplifier.

We first examine the circuit of amplifier A1. At point X1, $i_{T1} = -i_f$, and with application of Ohm's law, the value of e_{o1} is

$$e_{o1} = -R_f \left(\frac{e_1}{R_1} + \frac{e_2}{R_2} \right) \qquad \textbf{(4-2)}$$

The circuit of amplifier A2 can now be redrawn as shown in Fig. 4-3, with e_{ol} treated as an input. The output e_o is determined as before:

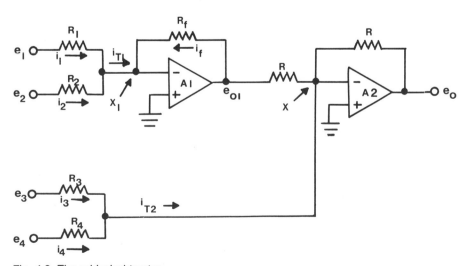

Fig. 4-2. The adder/subtractor.

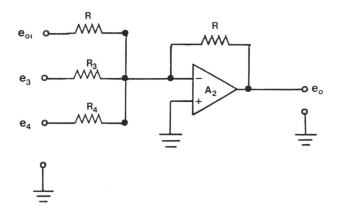

Fig. 4-3. Figure 4-2 (redrawn).

$$e_o = -R \left(\frac{e_{ol}}{R} + \frac{e_3}{R_3} + \frac{e_4}{R_4} \right) \qquad \textbf{(4-3)}$$

If we substitute the expression for e_{ol} (equation 4-2) into equation (4-3), we arrive at the expression for the output voltage e_o as a function of e_1, e_2, e_3, and e_4:

$$e_o = R_f \left(\frac{e_1}{R_1} + \frac{e_2}{R_2} \right) - R \left(\frac{e_3}{R_3} + \frac{e_4}{R_4} \right) \qquad \textbf{(4-4)}$$

Thus addition and subtraction are performed with one circuit, that of Fig. 4-2. Inputs to A1 are added, inputs to A2 are subtracted, and the output is given at e_o.

An obvious simplicity results if we set $R_f = R$. In that case, equation (4-4) becomes

$$e_o = R \left(\frac{e_1}{R_1} + \frac{e_2}{R_2} - \frac{e_3}{R_3} - \frac{e_4}{R_4} \right) \qquad \textbf{(4-5)}$$

That is what we will do in constructing the adder/subtractor module. The circuit is shown in Fig. 4-4. Again we make use of the dual 741-type op amp. Two 741 op amps may be used instead. Resistors R1 - R8 are added externally to scale the addition or subtraction. Positions 1 - 4 are used for addition, while positions 5 -

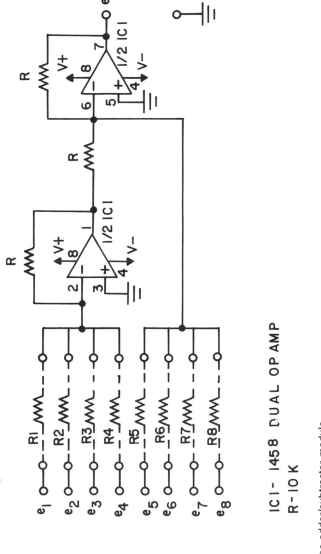

Fig. 4-4. The adder/subtractor module.

8 are used for subtraction. The output is given by equation (4-6).

$$e_o = R\left(\frac{e_1}{R_1} + \frac{e_2}{R_2} + \frac{e_3}{R_3} + \frac{e_4}{R_4} - \frac{e_5}{R_5} - \frac{e_6}{R_6} - \frac{e_7}{R_7} - \frac{e_8}{R_8}\right)$$ **(4-6)**

As with previous circuits, the circuit of Fig. 4-4 may be constructed on a universal breadboard socket for laboratory uses or fabricated on a universal IC board and enclosed in a plastic box for industrial applications. The physical appearance of the module is shown in Fig. 4-5, with terminal strips for resistor connections. Power supply connections are at the rear of the cabinet, as before.

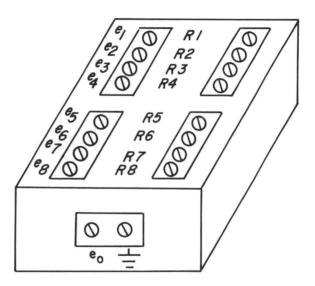

Fig. 4-5. Physical appearance of the adder/subtractor module.

Chapter 5

Multiplication, Division, Squares, and Square Roots

W E HAVE EXAMINED ONE FORM OF MULTIPLICATION IN Chapter 3, that of multiplication by constant coefficients. In this chapter we examine multiplication of variables, or quantities that change with time. This sort of multiplication is much more difficult to achieve than multiplication of a variable by a constant. Once multiplication has been achieved, however, we find that inclusion of a multiplier in a feedback loop permits division, squaring, and extraction of square roots.

MULTIPLICATION OF VARIABLES

There are several methods for performing analog multiplication. This section examines three of them: the logarithmic method, the quarter-square method, and the variable transconductance method.

The logarithmic method is conceptually simple and forms the basis for multiplication by the slide rule. Equation (5-1) describes the heart of the method: the *sum* of the logarithms of two voltages is equal to the logarithm of the *product* of the two voltages.

$$\log (e_1) + \log (e_2) = \log (e_1 \times e_2) \qquad \textbf{(5-1)}$$

35

The C and D scales of a slide rule (which are used for multiplication and division) are logarithmic scales. Multiplication (or division) on a slide rule simply involves sliding the C scale so as to add (or subtract) the logarithms of numbers. Electronically, this is achieved with the circuit of Fig. 5-1. Log amps and antilog amps are described in Chapter 7.

Division of variables can also be performed logarithmically, since the difference of the logarithms of two voltages is equal to the logarithm of the ratio of the two voltages:

$$\log\ (e_1)\ -\ \log\ (e_2)\ =\ \log\left(\frac{e_1}{e_2}\right) \qquad \textbf{(5-2)}$$

The difficulty with the logarithmic method of multiplication is readily apparent: the logarithms of negative numbers are undefined. Thus, multiplication (and division) by this method is restricted to positive values of e_1 and e_2 (i.e., one-quadrant multiplication). Also, the logarithm of zero is undefined, so one of the essential rules of multiplication cannot be satisfied with the logarithmic multiplier.

Four-quadrant operation (i.e., positive or negative values of e_1 and e_2) can be achieved with the quarter-square multiplier. The basis of the quarter-square multiplier is equation (5-3):

$$e_1\ \times\ e_2\ =\ 1/4\left[(e_1\ +\ e_2)^2\ -\ (e_1\ -\ e_2)^2\right] \qquad \textbf{(5-3)}$$

The procedure outlined in Fig. 5-2 can be followed to obtain the product of two voltages. The squarers shown in Fig. 5-2 are simple diode function generators.

As shown in Fig. 5-2, several amps and function generators are needed to obtain the product $e_1\ \times\ e_2$. This is a disadvantage of the quarter-square multiplier. Also, the percentage error of the quarter-square multiplier can be significant when e_1 is close in value to e_2.

The variable transconductance method of multiplication is the basis of most of the IC multipliers on the market today, and is shown in Fig. 5-3. The collector current i_c is given by equation (5-4), where B is a constant.

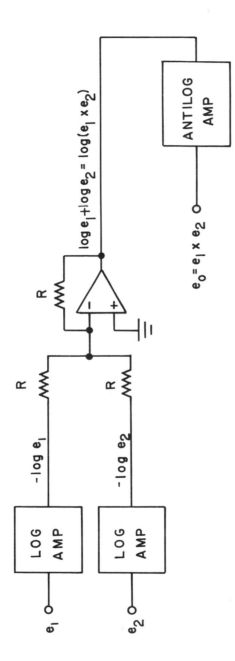

Fig. 5-1. Logarithmic method of multiplication.

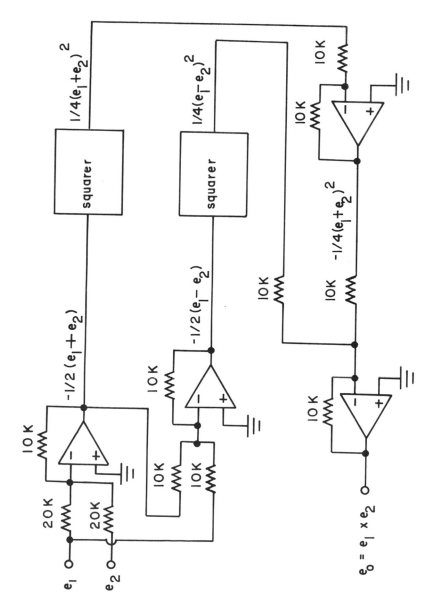

Fig. 5-2. Quarter-square method of multiplication.

$$i_c = B \times i_e \times e_1 \qquad \text{(5-4)}$$

If the emitter current i_e is set by e_2, and the collector current is converted to a voltage, then the output of the circuit of Fig. 5-3 is simply the product of two voltages times a scaling factor D:

$$e_o = D \times e_1 \times e_2 \qquad \text{(5-5)}$$

Of course, practical variable transconductance multipliers are more complicated than the circuit of Fig. 5-3; however, we will not examine them in detail. Readers interested in the specifics of those circuits will find the references in the bibliography quite useful. We will use an *analog multiplier IC*, which is an integrated circuit containing a variable transconductance multiplier and an op amp. This chip is relatively inexpensive and pro-

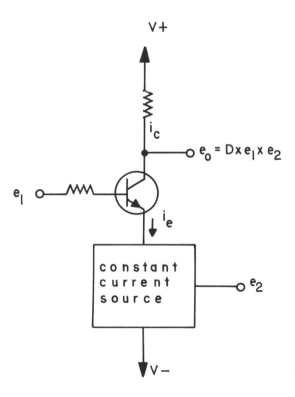

Fig. 5-3. Variable transconductance method of multiplication.

$$e_o = -k \times e_1 \times e_2$$
$$k = \text{scale factor}$$

Fig. 5-4. Schematic symbol for the analog multiplier.

vides a convenient way to perform multiplication, division, squaring, and the extraction of square roots. We will examine this IC in detail later in this chapter. For the time being, it will be convenient to represent the multiplier circuit (whether it be logarithmic, quarter-square, or variable transconductance) schematically by the symbol shown in Fig. 5-4.

DIVISION OF VARIABLES

Once multiplication has been achieved, division can be easily accomplished by including a multiplier in the feedback loop of an op amp. Such a circuit is shown in Fig. 5-5.

The output voltage of the multiplier is $e_{om} = -k \times e_1 \times e_2$. Since $e_2 = e_o$, e_{om} is actually a scaled multiple of the output and e_1:

$$e_{om} = -k \times e_o \times e_1 \qquad (5\text{-}6)$$

Since the op amp is ideal, with zero differential voltage, e_3 and e_{om} must sum to zero at point X, thus $e_{om} =$

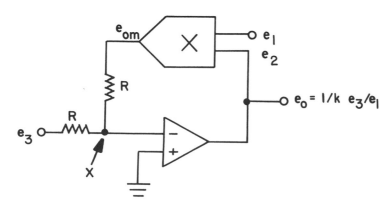

$$e_o = 1/k \ e_3/e_1$$

Fig. 5-5. Division.

$-e_3$. Substituting this into equation (5-6) yields

$$e_{om} = -k \times e_o \times e_1 = -e_3 \qquad \textbf{(5-7)}$$

and solving for e_o gives equation (5-8).

$$e_o = \frac{1}{K} \frac{e_3}{e_1} \qquad \textbf{(5-8)}$$

We see that using a multiplier in the feedback loop of an op amp provides a convenient method for performing division. This will be the method described in detail later in this chapter. The multiplier IC chosen for this purpose contains a multiplier, op amp, and two resistors in one chip, so that external connections are minimized.

SQUARES AND SQUARE ROOTS

Squaring a voltage is as simple an operation to perform as multiplication. The same voltage is fed into both input terminals of the multiplier and the output voltage is just the square of the input voltage times a scaling factor. This is shown in Fig. 5-6.

To extract square roots, we once again employ a multiplier in the feedback loop of an op amp. A circuit that extracts the square root of a number is shown in Fig. 5-7. This circuit is very similar to the divider circuit of Fig. 5-5, except that the same voltage is applied to both inputs of the multiplier.

Following our previous analysis, we see that $e_{om} = -ke_1{}^2$, and since $e_1 = e_o$, we have

$$e_{om} = -ke_o{}^2 \qquad \textbf{(5-9)}$$

Assuming that the op amp is ideal, e_{om} and e_3 must

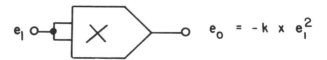

Fig. 5-6. Squaring a voltage.

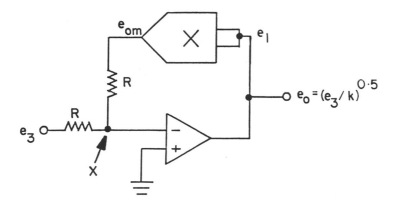

Fig. 5-7. Extracting the square root.

sum to zero at point X, thus

$$e_3 = ke_o^2 \qquad \textbf{(5-10)}$$

Solving equation (5-10) for e_o gives the output of the square rooter:

$$e_o = \sqrt{\frac{e_3}{k}} \qquad \textbf{(5-11)}$$

The use of a multiplier, op amp, and two resistors allows multiplication, division, squaring, and square rooting to be performed. As stated previously, we will employ a single IC that contains all the above components, thus simplifying the external connections required to perform all four operations.

THE IC MULTIPLIER

There are several IC multipliers on the market, including the MC 1495 (Motorola Semiconductor Products, Inc., P.O. Box 20912, Phoenix, AZ 85036) and the AD 532, AD 533, and AD 534 (Analog Devices, Two Technology Way, P.O. Box 280, Norwood, MA 02062 617/329-4700). Because of its low cost, simplicity of operation, good accuracy and four-quadrant operation, the author chose to work with the AD 533. Any multiplier can be used as long as technical data sheets are consulted to assure proper operation.

The AD 533 comes in two styles (TO-100 metal can or TO-116 ceramic DIP package) and three levels of accuracy (AD 533J, AD 533K, and AD 533L). Also, the AD 533 can be used over a wide temperature range (− 55 °C to + 125 °C for the AD 533S). The principle of operation and pinouts are the same for all versions of the AD 533 (given the same style package). It is recommended that the manufacturer be contacted regarding prices. A reproduction of the AD 533 data sheet is given in the Appendix.

The AD 533 is shown schematically in Fig. 5-8 in the multiplier configuration with external connections and potentiometers. The box marked with an X in Fig. 5-8 is the multiplier unit (as in Fig. 5-4). The multiplier is followed by an inverting amp so that the output is positive if two positive or two negative inputs are applied.

Multiplier operation requires closing the feedback loop around the op amp (by connecting Z_{in} to V_o) and by proper trimming. Trim procedure for multiplication

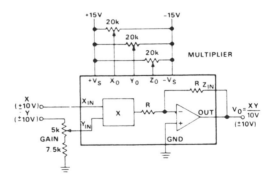

TRIM PROCEDURES

1. With $X = Y = 0$ volts, adjust Z_0 for 0V dc output.
2. With $Y = 20$ volts p-p (at $f = 50Hz$) and $X = 0V$, adjust X_0 for minimum ac output.
3. With $X = 20$ volts p-p (at $f = 50Hz$) and $Y = 0V$, adjust Y_0 for minimum ac output.
4. Readjust Z_0 for 0V dc output.
5. With $X = +10V$ dc and $Y = 20$ volts p-p (at $f = 50Hz$), adjust gain for output $= Y_{in}$.

NOTE: For best accuracy over limited voltage ranges (e.g., ±5V), gain and feedthrough adjustments should be optimized with the inputs in the desired range, as linearity is considerably better over smaller ranges of input.

Fig. 5-8. Multiplication with the AD 533 (reprinted with permission of Analog Devices, Inc.).

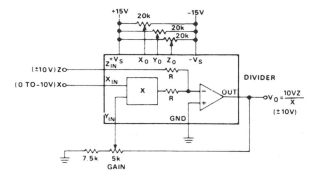

TRIM PROCEDURES

1. Set all pots at mid-scale.
2. With Z = 0V, trim Z_0 to hold the output constant, as X is varied from −10V dc through −1V dc.
3. With Z = 0V, X = −10V dc, trim Y_0 for 0V dc.
4. With Z = X or −X, trim X_0 for the minimum worst-case variations as X is varied from −10V dc to −1V dc.
5. Repeat steps 2 and 3 if step 4 required a large initial adjustment.
6. With Z = X or −X, trim the gain for the closest average approach to ± 10V dc output as X is varied from −10V dc to −3V dc.

Fig. 5-9. Division with the AD 533 (reprinted with permission of Analog Devices, Inc.).

is given in Fig. 5-8, and involves balancing the X and Y input channels to minimize feedthrough of Y and X, respectively. Also, the Z_o null potentiometer compensates for op amp offset voltage, and the gain potentiometer sets full scale level. As can be seen from the figure, multiplication is four-quadrant (X and Y can be either positive or negative). Maximum input voltages are ± 10 V and maximum output voltage is ± 10 V. The output voltage is equal to the product of the input voltages divided by 10 V:

$$v_o = k \times X \times Y; \ k = 0.1 \text{ V} \qquad \textbf{(5-12)}$$

A circuit for division using the AD 533 is shown in Fig. 5-9. This is just the circuit of Fig. 5-5 with the addition of null and full-scale gain potentiometers. Only two-quadrant division is allowed; i.e., Z may be either positive or negative, but X must be negative. The accuracy and bandwidth of this circuit decreases as X decreases. The output voltage is equal to Z divided by X, times 10 V;

$$v_o = \frac{1}{k} \frac{Z;}{X} \quad k = 0.1\,V \qquad \text{(5-13)}$$

A circuit which performs the squaring operation using the AD 533 is shown in Fig. 5-10, and is the same circuit as that shown in Fig. 5-6. The X and Y inputs are connected (through the gain potentiometer) and the result is the square of the input voltage divided by 10 V:

$$v_o = k\,X^2; \quad k = 0.1\,V \qquad \text{(5-14)}$$

Since the X and Y inputs are connected, only the X_o null potentiometer is needed. Trim procedure is shown in Fig. 5-10.

A circuit that extracts the square root using the AD 533 is shown in Fig. 5-11, and is equivalent to the circuit of Fig. 5-7. The X and Y inputs are tied together

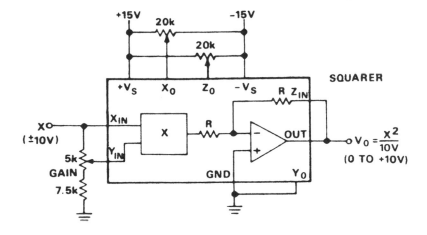

TRIM PROCEDURES
1. With X = 0 volts, adjust Z_0 for 0V dc output.
2. With X = +10V dc, adjust gain for +10V dc output.
3. Reverse polarity of X input and adjust X_0 to reduce the output error to ½ its original value, readjust the gain to take out the remaining error.
4. Check the output offset with input grounded. If nonzero, repeat the above procedure until no errors remain.

Fig. 5-10. Squaring with the AD 533 (reprinted with permission of Analog Devices, Inc.).

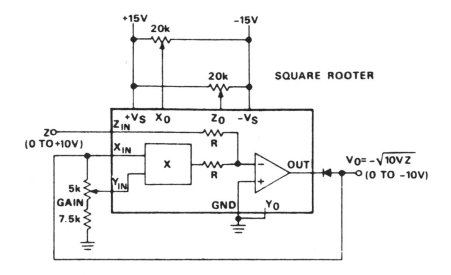

TRIM PROCEDURES

1. With Z = +0.1 V dc, adjust Z_0 for Output = –1.0V dc.
2. With Z = +10.0V dc, adjust gain for Output = –10.0V dc.
3. With Z = +2.0V dc, adjust X_0 for Output = –4.47 ±0.1 V dc.
4. Repeat steps 2 and 3, if necessary. Repeat step 1.

Fig. 5-11. Extracting the square root with the AD 533 (reprinted with permission of Analog Devices, Inc.).

through the gain potentiometer, so that the Y_o null potentiometer is not needed. Inputs are restricted to positive values, and the output is the negative square root Z times 10 V:

$$v_o = -\sqrt{\frac{Z}{k}} \; ; \quad k = 0.1V \qquad \textbf{(5-15)}$$

Trim procedure is shown in Fig. 5-11. The external diode prevents latch-up.

We have seen that the AD 533 is a low cost versatile multiplier requiring a minimum number of external components. The next section will describe a circuit that allows the AD 533 to be converted quickly from one configuration to another.

THE MULTIPLIER MODULE

A circuit that capitalizes on the AD 533's flexibil-

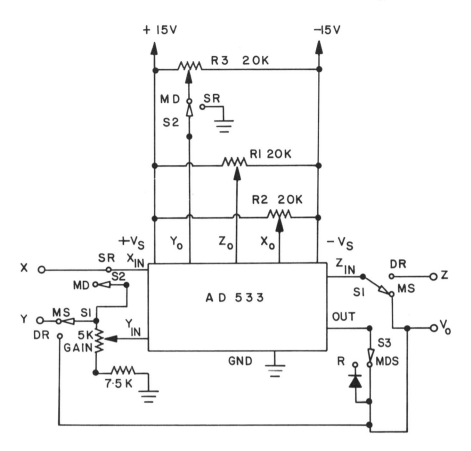

Fig. 5-12. The multiplier module.

ity yet allows the circuit to be enclosed in a durable box is shown in Fig. 5-12. The circuit requires four potentiometers, three switches, a resistor and a diode. S1 and S2 are DPDT switches and S3 is a SPDT switch. When all three switches are in the M position, the unit is ready to be trimmed for multiplication. Likewise, when all switches are in the D, S, and R positions, the unit is ready to be trimmed for division, squaring, and square rooting, respectively. The AD 533 is conveniently mounted on a universal IC board along with the diode and 7.5 kΩ resistor. R1, R2, R3, 5kΩ gain potentiometer, S1, S2, and S3 are mounted on the front panel of the box, as shown in Fig. 5-13. As with previous modules, power supply connections are at the rear of the cabinet.

Multiplication, Division, Squares, and Square Roots

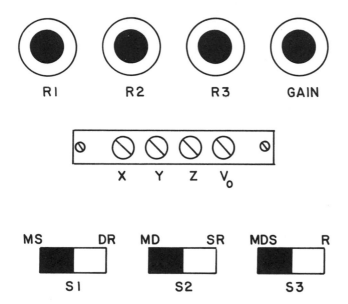

Fig. 5-13. Front view of multiplier module.

Chapter 6

Integration and Differentiation

IN THIS CHAPTER WE CONSIDER THE MATHEMATICAL OPERA-
tions of integration and differentiation, and how they
are performed with analog computational circuits. Integration can be viewed as finding the area under a
curve. If we have a voltage e which varies with time t,
the integral I of that voltage from time $t = 0$ to some
other time $t = t_o$ is given by equation (6-1):

$$I = \int_{t=0}^{t=t_o} e \, dt \qquad \textbf{(6-1)}$$

where dt is an infinitesimally small increment of time.
In short, the product of voltage e and time interval dt
is summed from $t = 0$ to $t = t_o$. As shown in Fig. 6-1,
this yields the area under the $e - t$ curve.

Differentiation is the opposite of integration. It is
the change in e divided by the infinitesimally small
change in t, and is represented by the symbol de/dt.
If the changes in t are small enough, the derivative of
e with respect to t is approximately equal to the change
in e divided by the change in t:

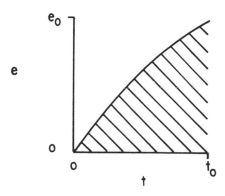

Fig. 6-1. Integration as the area under a curve.

$$\frac{de}{dt} \cong \frac{\Delta e}{\Delta t} \qquad \qquad (6\text{-}2)$$

The derivative de/dt is just the slope of the $e - t$ curve in Fig. 6-1 at a given point, or the slope of a line tangent to the point of interest.

Differential equations are equations containing derivatives, so their solutions will involve integration. We will examine the ideal integrator in the next section.

THE IDEAL INTEGRATOR

The ideal integrator is shown in Fig. 6-2. This circuit is simply an op amp with a capacitor in the feedback loop and a resistor connected to the inverting input. The voltage across the feedback capacitor C is e_o, and it is related to the capacitor current i_f by equation (6-3):

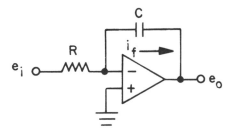

Fig. 6-2. The ideal integrator.

50

$$e_o = \frac{-1}{C} \int_{t=0}^{t=t_o} i_f \, dt \qquad \text{(6-3)}$$

Assuming that the op amp is ideal, i_f is equal to the input current, which is just e_i/R. Substituting this into equation (6-3) gives us the output voltage of the integrator as a function of input voltage.

$$e_o = -\frac{1}{RC} \int_{t=0}^{t=t_o} e_i \, dt \qquad \text{(6-4)}$$

In other words, the output voltage is equal to the integral of the input voltage scaled by the factor $-1/RC$.

As you might have guessed, the ideal integrator does not exist. Deviations from the ideal cause special problems that must be addressed. These are discussed in the next section.

THE NONIDEAL INTEGRATOR

Let us assume that a constant voltage of $e_i = 1$ volt is applied to the integrator of Fig. 6-2. Further, let us assume that $C = 1$ microfarad and $R = 1$ megohm, so that $RC = 1$ second. Since e_i is constant, it can be pulled outside the integral sign in equation 6-4. The solution then becomes

$$e_o = -\frac{e_i}{RC} \int_{t=0}^{t=t_o} dt = \frac{e_i}{RC} (t_o - 0) = -t_o \text{ volts} \qquad \text{(6-5)}$$

since $e_i = 1$ volt and $RC = (10^{-6}F \times 10^6 \text{ ohms}) = 1$ second. The output voltage will equal the length of time (in seconds) that the integrator is operating.

What happens if we let the integrator run for 20 seconds? According to equation (6-5), the output will be -20 volts, but that cannot happen since our op amp will saturate at around ± 12 volts. The output given by equation (6-5) and the actual output are shown in Fig. 6-3. Thus, the first restriction on the use of the integrator shown in Fig. 6-2 is that the time scale for integration must be set to avoid saturating the op amp. The time

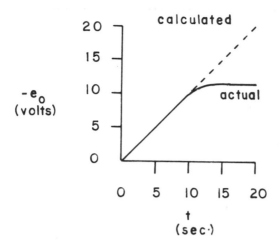

Fig. 6-3. Actual and calculated integrator output.

scale is selected by appropriate choice of values for R and C.

If we need to use the integrator for 20 seconds, we could pick C = 1 microfarad and R = 2 megohms. Equation (6-5) would then become

$$e_o = - \frac{t_o}{2} \text{ volts} \tag{6-6}$$

and at 20 seconds the output would be – 10 volts. Saturation of the op amp would then be avoided.

Input offset voltage and bias current are more serious errors in integrators than in other op amp circuits since the integrator sums the errors while operating. When considering these effects, the output of the integrator is given by equation (6-7):

$$e_o = - \frac{1}{RC} \int e_i dt + \frac{1}{RC} \int e_{io} dt + \frac{1}{C} \int i_b dt + e_{io} \tag{6-7}$$

where e_{io} and i_b are the input offset voltage and bias current, respectively. The largest error term in equation (6-7) is the term involving i_b since it is multiplied by the inverse of C, and C is in microfarads (10^{-6}F). This term can be decreased by increasing the value of C, which will require a decrease in R for a fixed time scale. Decreasing R lowers the input impedance of the integrator, so there is a lower limit on the value of R. Good quality capacitors above 1 - 5 microfarads are available; however, they are bulky and expensive. Also, the insulation resistance of a capacitor generally decreases as its capacitance increases. We want the insulation resistance as high as possible because the capacitor's leakage current must be kept below the op amp's bias current.

The next section will describe practical integrators in which the aforementioned considerations have been addressed.

THE PRACTICAL INTEGRATOR

The first consideration in designing a practical integrator is the choice of an op amp. This will be governed in part by the length of computing time and desired accuracy.

Our old standby, the 741 op amp, is practically worthless as an integrator except for very short computing times. A glance at its data sheet explains why this is so. Its input offset voltage is typically 2.0 mV, which is not bad. Its input bias current, however, is typically 80 nA (80 $\times$ 10^{-9}A), and can be as high as 500 nA. In our previous example, with e_i = 1 V, R = 2 megohms and C = 1 microfarad, a twenty second integration would yield e_o = $-$ 10 V + 1.622 V (assuming e_{io} = 2.0 mV and i_b = 80 nA). This amounts to an error of 16.22%, of which 16% is due to the input bias current.

This error gets worse as integration time lengthens. For an integration time of 1 minute (with a 6-megohm resistor to prevent saturation), the total error would be 48.22%, of which 48 % is due to the input bias current.

A better device for long integration time is the FET input op amp. An example of this is the LF 353 dual-JFET-input op amp by National Semiconductor. Because of its JFET input, it has extremely high input impedance (10^{-12} ohms, compared to 2 $\times$ 10^6 ohms for the 741). This results in a very small input bias current (50 $\times$ 10^{12}A, compared to 80 $\times$ 10^{-9}A for the 741). Using the LF 353 in the previous example, a 20 second integration would result in an error of 0.12%, of which 0.01% is due to input bias current. For a 60 second integration, the error is 0.14%, of which 0.03% is due to input bias current.

The op amp best suited for long-term integrations is the *chopper-stabilized op amp*, which is characterized by low input offset voltage and bias current, and by superior long-term dc stability. The details of chopper-stabilization can be found in the references in the bibliography. The disadvantage of the chopper-stabilized op amp is its price. The cheaper ones cost more than $70, while the more expensive ones cost $200 apiece. By contrast, the LF 353 is a dual-JFET op amp (two amps in one package) that costs less than $3. The reader interested in chopper-stabilized op amps is advised to examine the Model 234 or Model 235 op amp from Analog Devices.

In the construction of our integrator, we will use the LF 353 because of its low cost, wide availability (it can be purchased at Radio Shack), high input impedance and low bias current.

Having established the type of op amp to be used, we now examine a practical integrator circuit, which is shown in Fig. 6-4. The output e_o for this circuit (excluding error terms) is given by equation (6-8):

$$e_o = \frac{1}{RC} \int_{t=0}^{t=t_o} e_i \, dt + \text{I.C.} \qquad \textbf{(6-8)}$$

where I.C. indicates the *initial conditions*, or the voltage applied to the capacitor before beginning integration. In the example of the ideal integrator, Fig. 6-2, the initial condition was $e_o = 0$ volts at a time $t = 0$ (since the capacitor was initially uncharged).

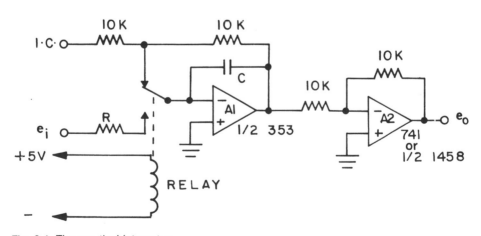

Fig. 6-4. The practical integrator.

the capacitor was initially uncharged).

Amplifier A1 is one of the JFET input op amps in the LF 353, with high input impedance and low bias current to minimize the errors associated with integration. While the relay is not energized, the initial condition voltage is applied through the two 10 kΩ resistors. These resistors, together with A1, form an inverting amplifier which charges C to the negative value of the initial condition voltage applied at the I.C. terminal. When the relay is energized, and integration begins, the input voltage is applied through R and the output of amplifier A1 is given by equation (6-9):

$$e_{oA1} = - \frac{1}{RC} \int_{t=0}^{t=t_0} e_i dt - \text{I.C.} \tag{6-9}$$

Amplifier A2 is an inverting amplifier with unity gain. The output of A2 is given by equation (6-8), which is just the negative of equation (6-9). The 741 op amp, or one of the op amps in the 1458 dual op amp, may be used for this amplifier.

The time scale of integration is set by the product of R and C. The choice of these values, however, deserves special mention. The quality of the feedback capacitor C is a limiting factor in op amp integrator accuracy. We have seen that the larger the value of C, the smaller the contribution of the input bias current error term. The capacitor's leakage current must be lower than the bias current for the op amp, which is typically 50 pA for the LF 353. Polystyrene, polypropylene, Teflon, polycarbonate, and polyester capacitors are excellent choices for C, since their leakage currents are in the pA range. Capacitors with values above 1 – 5 microfarads are physically large and very expensive. It is recommended that a high quality polystyrene, Teflon, or polypropylene capacitor in the range of 1 – 5 microfarads be selected for integration and that the capacitor be permanently mounted in the integrator. The time constant will then be set by R.

The optimum value of R (i.e., that value that minimizes effects of bias current and input offset voltage) is given by e_{io}/i_b, which is typically 20 megohms for the LF 353. This is fine from the standpoint that it provides sufficient input impedance to prevent loading other circuits; however, it must be remembered that the availability of precision resistors above 10 megohms is somewhat limited, so some latitude in the choice of R is needed. The lower limit on R is that R must be large enough to prevent loading the previous stage.

The circuit of Fig. 6-4 will be the integrator we use to solve differential equations. In the next section we discuss differentiation (the opposite of integration) and how it is performed with analog computational circuits.

THE IDEAL DIFFERENTIATOR

Since we have stated that differentiation is the opposite mathematical operation from integration, you might well imagine that the ideal differentiator circuit is just that of Fig. 6-2 but with the capacitor and resistor switched. That is in fact the case, as shown in Fig. 6-5. The input current, expressed in terms of C and e_i, is given by equation (6-10).

$$i_{in} = C \frac{de_i}{dt} \qquad \text{(6-10)}$$

Assuming that the op amp is ideal, no current flows into the noninverting input. The currents at point X must then sum to zero, or $i_{in} = -i_f$. Since $i_f = e_o/R$, we have

$$C \frac{de_i}{dt} = -\frac{e_o}{R} \qquad \text{(6-11)}$$

or

$$e_o = -RC \frac{de_i}{dt} \qquad \text{(6-12)}$$

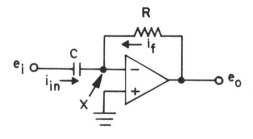

Fig. 6-5. The ideal differentiator.

In other words, the output voltage is equal to the derivative with respect to time of the input voltage, scaled by the factor $-RC$.

It is apparent that the derivative of a constant is zero. With a capacitive input, a constant (dc) e_i would not be passed and e_o would be zero. The input voltage e_i must be varying in order to have a nonzero output voltage.

As with the ideal integrator, the ideal differentiator does not exist. The deviations from ideality and how they are addressed are covered in the next section.

THE NONIDEAL DIFFERENTIATOR

The nonideal behavior of the differentiator is caused by the finite gain and finite bandwidth of the nonideal op amp. The circuit of Fig. 6-5 has a gain that increases with frequency (at the rate of 20 dB per decade, or 6 dB per octave). Since gain increases with frequency, the differentiator is susceptible to high frequency noise. Also, the RC network around the op amp introduces a 90° phase shift which gives the circuit a tendency to oscillate. The circuit of Fig. 6-5 is thus noisy and unstable.

These two problems can be corrected with the circuit of Fig. 6-6. The input resistor R_i is used to limit the high frequency gain, thus cutting down on differentiator noise. The feedback capacitor C_f helps stabilize the differentiator. The 90° phase lag of RC is compensated with a 90° phase lead of R_iC and RC_f. This reduces loop instability and minimizes the tendency of the differentiator to oscillate.

How do we choose the values of R_i, C, R, and C_f? These values are generally determined by the input fre-

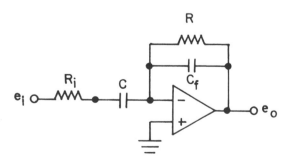

Fig. 6-6. The practical differentiator.

quency to the differentiator. If f is the highest frequency input to the differentiator, then the following formulae may be used:

$$R_i = \frac{0.316}{2\pi f C} \qquad \textbf{(6-13)}$$

and

$$C_f = \frac{1}{2\pi f R} \qquad \textbf{(6-14)}$$

Equation (6-13) gives the minimum value of R_i required for stability. A higher value is satisfactory. Equation (6-14) simply states that the reactance of C_f is equal to that of R at frequency f. The limitation on the op amp is given by equation (6-15):

$$f_{max} = \sqrt{\frac{GBW}{20\pi RC}} \qquad \textbf{(6-15)}$$

Where GBW is the *gain-bandwidth product* of the op amp. For the LF 353, the GBW is typically 4 MHz. Thus, with R = 1 megohm and C = 1 microfarad, the LF 353 can be used accurately up to a frequency of 250 Hz. Decreasing R increases f_{max}.

In designing the practical differentiator, we will use the same high quality polystyrene, Teflon, or polypropylene capacitor chosen for the integrator as C. The input resistance R_i will then be set by the frequency of the input, as given by equation (6-13). The choice of R will be limited by equation (6-15), and C_f will be chosen according to equation (6-14).

THE INTEGRATOR-DIFFERENTIATOR MODULE

A circuit that can be used either as an integrator or differentiator is given in Fig. 6-7. This is the circuit we will build and enclose in a plastic or metal box. Switch S1 is a double-pole double-throw switch, which when closed is in the integrate position and when open is in the differentiate position. The relay in Fig. 6-7 is shown in the de-energized position.

To integrate, S1 is closed and a resistor is connected

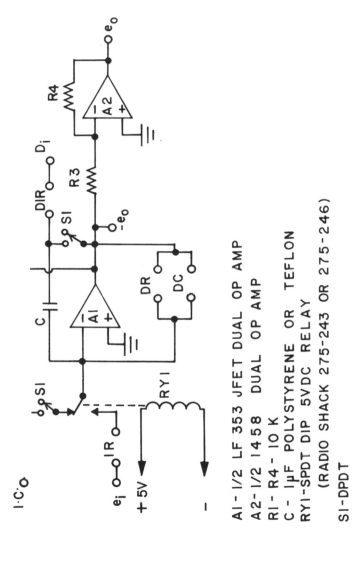

A1 - 1/2 LF 353 JFET DUAL OP AMP
A2 - 1/2 1458 DUAL OP AMP
R1 - R4 - 10 K
C - 1μF POLYSTYRENE OR TEFLON
RY1-SPDT DIP 5VDC RELAY
(RADIO SHACK 275-243 OR 275-246)

S1-DPDT

Fig. 6-7. The integrator-differentiator module.

across the IR terminals. DIR, DR, and DC positions are left vacant. The initial condition is applied at the IC terminal and the input to the integrator is applied at the e_i terminal. Integration begins when the relay is energized and ends when the relay is de-energized. The output at the $-e_o$ terminal is given by equation (6-9) (where $-e_o = e_{oA1}$) and the output at the e_o terminal is given by equation (6-8).

To differentiate, S1 is open, IR is left vacant, and appropriate values of R_i, R, and C_f (Fig. 6-6) are connected across the DIR, DR, and DC terminals, respectively. The input to the differentiator is applied at the D_i terminal. The output at the $-e_o$ terminal is $-RCde_i/dt$ and the output at the e_o terminal is given by equation (6-16).

$$e_o = RC\,\frac{de_i}{dt} \qquad \textbf{(6-16)}$$

Since we are using only half of the LF 353 and 1458,

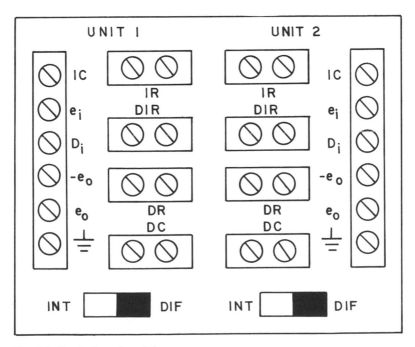

Fig. 6-8. Front view of module.

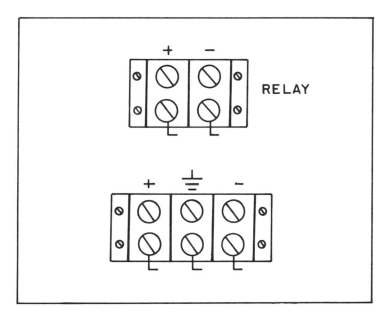

Fig. 6-9. Power supply connections at rear.

two integrator-differentiator circuits can be enclosed in a single box. Fabrication on a universal IC board is recommended. The physical appearance of the integrator-differentiator module is shown in Fig. 6-8. As before, power supply connections are made at the rear of the cabinet (Fig. 6-9).

Chapter 7

Function Generation

T HE GENERATION OF FUNCTIONS OF VARIABLES IS AN IMPOR-
tant process in solving difficult differential equations. This chapter considers the four most common
functions encountered in differential equations: the logarithm, the antilogarithm (or exponential), the sine and
the cosine functions. A host of other functions, which
are generated through a process known as implicit generation, will be studied in the next chapter.

LOGARITHM GENERATION

The ideal logarithm (or log) generator is very simple, and is shown in Fig. 7-1. It involves the use of a
simple bipolar transistor or diode in the feedback network of an op amp. When the collector-base voltage of
a silicon transistor is zero, its base-emitter voltage e_{BE}
is given by equation (7-1):

$$e_{BE} = \frac{kT}{q} \ln \left(\frac{i_c}{i_s} \right) \qquad (7\text{-}1)$$

where k = Boltzmann's constant = 1.3806×10^{-23}
J/°K

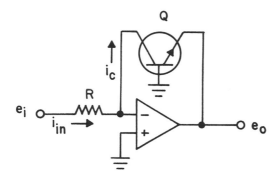

Fig. 7-1. Ideal log generator.

T = temperature (degrees Kelvin)
q = charge of an electron = 1.6022×10^{-19} C
ln = natural logarithm ($\log_e$)
i_c = collector current
i_s = emitter saturation current ($\cong 10^{-13}$A)

Since the op amp in Fig. 7-1 is considered ideal, the collector voltage is zero and equation (7-1) holds true for the transistor in the feedback loop. Also, because of the ideal behavior of the op amp, the input current i_{in} is equal to the collector current i_c. Since the output voltage is just equal to $-e_{BE}$, equation (7-1) becomes

$$e_o = -\frac{kT}{q} \; ln \left(\frac{i_c}{i_s} \right) \qquad \text{(7-2)}$$

As $i_c = i_{in} = e_i/R$, equation (7-2) becomes

$$e_o = -\frac{kT}{q} \; ln \left(\frac{e_i}{i_s R} \right) \qquad \text{(7-3)}$$

In other words, the output voltage e_o is equal to the logarithm of the ratio $e_i/i_s R$, scaled by the factor $-kT/q$.

Logarithms to the base 10, symbolized by $\log_{10}$, can be obtained from the natural logarithm ln by the following relationship:

$$\ln(e) = 2.303 \log_{10}(e) \qquad \textbf{(7-4)}$$

The circuit of Fig. 7-1 has two principal drawbacks: (1) the emitter saturation current i_s varies from transistor to transistor, so i_s is not always known, and (2) the circuit is temperature-dependent.

Compensation for i_s involves a property of logarithms that is very useful: the difference of two logarithms is equal to the logarithm of their ratio.

$$\ln(x) - \ln(y) = \ln\left(\frac{x}{y}\right) \qquad \textbf{(7-5)}$$

The way this property is used to compensate for i_s is shown in Fig. 7-2.

Two log amps are involved, the second of which is fed by a known reference voltage e_{ref}. The reference amp output is subtracted from the other log amp output, yielding equation (7-6).

$$e_o = -\frac{kT}{q}\left\{\ln\left(\frac{e_i}{i_s R}\right) - \ln\left(\frac{e_{ref}}{i_s R}\right)\right\} = -\frac{kT}{q}\ln\left(\frac{e_i}{e_{ref}}\right) \qquad \textbf{(7-6)}$$

In this way, the unknown voltage $i_s R$ is replaced with a controlled and known voltage e_{ref}. Obviously, the two transistors used in the log amps should be a matched pair.

The temperature-dependence of the log amp comes from the kT/q scaling factor. This factor changes by approximately $+0.3\%$ per change in degree Kelvin. Temperature compensation can be achieved by using a thermistor (with a temperature coefficient of $+0.3\%/°K$) as shown in Fig. 7-3.

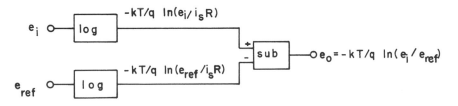

Fig. 7-2. Compensation for i_s.

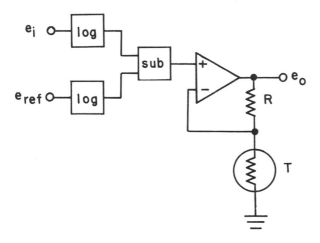

Fig. 7-3. Temperature compensation of log generator.

Figures 7-1, 7-2, and 7-3 are all that is needed to build a practical log generator. A more convenient method of building a log generator is to use *precision log modules*, which are temperature- and i_s - compensated log circuits prepackaged in epoxy encapsulated modules. The physical size of these modules is small (not much bigger than an IC), and the cost is not prohibitive (approximately $50, which compares favorably with the cost of precision components necessary to build the circuit of Fig. 7-3). These modules require only one external component (a trimming potentiometer) and are extremely flexible. The precision log module is thus an economical alternative to home construction. This module will be discussed in detail later in this chapter.

ANTILOGARITHM GENERATION

The generation of antilogarithms (or exponentials) is the inverse operation of log generation, and is performed by switching the position of the transistor and resistor in Fig. 7-1. A practical circuit for generating antilogarithms is shown in Fig. 7-4.

The input voltage e_i is applied across the $R - R_T$ voltage divider. Thus the input to the base of Q1 is $(R_T/R + R_T)e_i$. The voltage at the emitter of Q1 is the sum of the base and base-emitter voltage:

$$e_{eQ1} = \frac{R_T}{R + R_T} \quad e_i \quad - \quad \frac{kT}{q} \quad \ln \left(\frac{e_{ref}}{R_1 i_s}\right) \quad (7\text{-}7)$$

Since the emitter voltage of Q1 is applied to the collector of Q2, $e_{eQ1} = e_{BEQ2}$, so that equation (7-7) becomes

$$- \frac{kT}{q} \ln \left(\frac{e_o}{R_1 i_s}\right) = \frac{R_T}{R + R_T} \quad e_i \quad - \quad \frac{kT}{q} \quad \ln \left(\frac{e_{ref}}{R_1 i_s}\right) (7\text{-}8)$$

Rearranging equation (7-8) results in equation (7-9):

$$- \frac{q}{kT} \frac{R_T}{R + R_T} \quad e_i \quad = \quad \ln \left(\frac{e_o}{e_{ref}}\right) \quad (7\text{-}9)$$

It is easier to work with base 10 logarithm at this point. Recalling equation (7-4), we can rewrite equation (7-9) in terms of base 10 logarithms:

$$- Ke_i \quad = \quad \log_{10} \left(\frac{e_o}{e_{ref}}\right) \quad (7\text{-}10)$$

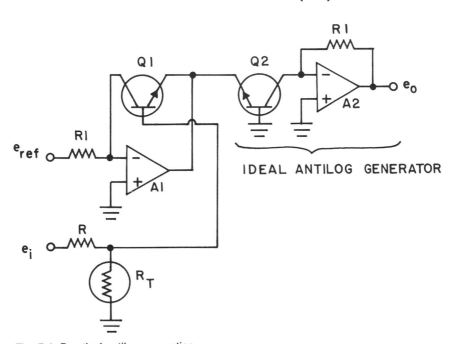

Fig. 7-4. Practical antilog generation.

where $K = qR_T/2.303kT(R + R_T)$. To arrive at an expression for e_o, we exponentiate both sides of equation (7-10). Recalling that $10^{(\log_{10}x)} = x$, we have

$$e_o = e_{ref}\, 10^{-Ke_i} \qquad\qquad \textbf{(7-11)}$$

In other words, the output of A2 is the scaled antilogarithm of e_i.

The circuit of Fig. 7-4 corrects for both i_s and temperature. As with the log generator, however, we will not build the circuit of Fig. 7-4. Instead, we will use the precision log module for generating antilogarithms. The circuit of Fig. 7-4 is already fabricated and enclosed in the log module, and requires only one trimming potentiometer for use.

THE PRECISION LOG-ANTILOG AMPLIFIER MODULE

As stated previously, log-antilog modules are available which perform both functions with a minimum of external components. The models 759N/P and 755N/P wideband log-antilog amplifiers from Analog Devices are two such modules. The model 755 is identical with the model 759, except that it has improved accuracy and costs twice as much. The designation N or P stands for NPN or PNP, respectively. Model 755N computes the log of positive input signals, while the 755P computes the log of negative input signals. In antilog operations, both the N and P versions accept bipolar input signals, but the output of the 755N is positive, while the output of the 755P is negative.

Since there are no differences in size, pinout or trimming procedures between the 755 and 759, we will discuss one of the models. It is assumed that the price of the 759 will make it an attractive alternative to the more accurate 755, so we will use the model 759N in the discussions that follow. The specifications of the two models are listed in the Appendix for purposes of comparison.

A block diagram of the 759N is shown in Fig. 7-5. It has nine pins, three of which are power supply connections and one of which is used to trim offset voltage. The five remaining pins (1 - 5 in Fig. 7-5) are inputs and outputs to and from the op amp and antilog element.

The antilog element of the 759 is very similar to the circuit of Fig. 7-4 (excluding A2 and its feedback resis-

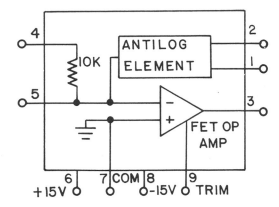

Fig. 7-5. Block diagram of the Model 759 (reprinted with permission of Analog Devices, Inc.).

tor). Perhaps the best way to visualize the antilog element is to ignore the i_s- and temperature-compensation circuits and treat the antilog element as a silicon transistor. This is shown in Fig. 7-6. When pin 1 is connected to pin 3, and the input is provided through pin 4, the circuit is a log amp with output at pin 3 (compare with Fig. 7-1). When the input is provided at pin 1, and pin 4 is connected to the output (pin 3), the circuit is an antilog amp (compare with the Q2-A2 portion of Fig. 7-4).

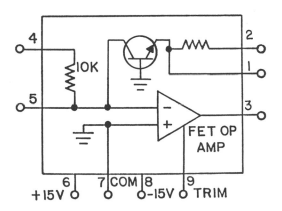

Fig. 7-6. Simplified diagram of the Model 759.

LOG OPERATION OF THE MODEL 759

The model 759 can be used in two ways to generate logarithms of inputs: the input can be a voltage (in which case the input is to pin 4), or the input can be a current (in which case the input is to pin 5). Since we have dealt with input and output voltages to this point, the operation of the 759 will be described for input voltages. The corresponding procedures for currents may be found in the data sheet (see Appendix).

Figure 7-7 shows the model 759 in the logarithmic mode. Pin 1 is connected to the output (pin 3) to complete the feedback loop, and the input voltage is applied to pin 4. A ten-turn 100 kΩ potentiometer is connected across the power supply terminals (pins 6 and 8) with the wiper connected to the trim pin (pin 9). Procedure for offset voltage trimming will be covered later.

The output in this configuration is given by equation (7-12):

$$e_o = - \, K\log_{10}\left(\frac{e_i}{e_{ref}}\right) \qquad \textbf{(7-12)}$$

where e_{ref} is an internally-generated reference voltage to compensate for i_s. The value of e_{ref} is just equal to

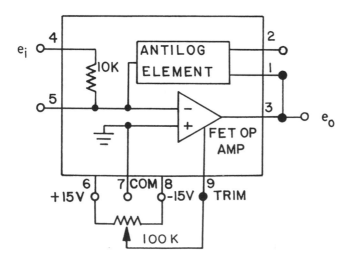

Fig. 7-7. Model 759 in the log mode (reprinted with permission of Analog Devices, Inc.).

the internally-generated reference current times the 10 kΩ resistance, or e_{ref} = 0.1 V (since i_{ref} = 10 microamps). The reference current (and hence the value of e_{ref}) may be changed by injecting a constant current into pin 2 (or pin 1, if pin 2 is used in the feedback loop). The injected current i_i necessary to achieve a desired reference current is given by equation (7-13).

$$i_i = (3.30 \times 10^{-4}A) \log_{10} \left(\frac{10^{-5}A}{i_{ref\ desired}} \right) \qquad (7\text{-}13)$$

Another way to change e_{ref} is to use a different value input resistance. To do this, pin 4 is disconnected and the input voltage is applied through an external resistor to pin 5. In this case the reference voltage becomes

$$e_{ref} = R_{ext} \times i_{ref} \qquad (7\text{-}14)$$

where i_{ref} = 10 microamps. If this is done, care should be taken so that $e_i(max)/R_{ext} \leq 1$ mA.

The constant K in equation (7-12) is a scale factor and is set during the trimming of the log amp and by choice of feedback pins (1 or 2).

The amplifier is usually trimmed to obtain an offset of 100 microvolts or less. The procedure is as follows. Ground the input pin (pin 4, unless an input current or external resistor is used). If e_{ref} = 0.1 V, and K = 1 is desired, then adjust the ten turn 100 kΩ potentiometer until e_o is + 3 volts or greater (if using the 759N) or – 3 volts or greater (if using the 759P). For a different value of K, the following formula should be used to set the lower value of e_o:

$$e_o = -K\log_{10} \left(\frac{1 \times 10^{-4}}{e_{ref}} \right) \qquad (7\text{-}15)$$

Another way to change the value of K is to connect pin 2 to pin 3 (instead of pin 1 to pin 3). This will give K = 2. Also, resistors connected between pins 1 or 2 and pin 3 can be used to adjust K. The values of the resistors, and the pins to which they are connected, are given in Table 7-1.

In the log mode, input voltages for the 759N can

**Table 7-1. Resistor Selection Chart for Shifting
Scale Factor (Reprinted with Permission of Analog Devices, Inc.)**

Range of K	Connect Series R to Pin	Value of R
2/3 V to 1.01 V	1	$3K\Omega \times (K - 2/3)$
1.01 V to 2.02 V	1	$3K\Omega \times (K - 1)$
>2.02 V	2	$3K\Omega \times (K - 2)$

range between $+1$ mV to $+10$ V (-1 mV to -10 V for the 759P). Output voltage range is ± 10 V.

ANTILOG OPERATION OF THE MODEL 759

Antilog operation is shown in Fig. 7-8. The feed-back loop around the op amp is completed by connecting pin 4 to the output (pin 3). The voltage input is applied to either pin 1 (K = 1) or pin 2 (K = 2). Adjustment of the scale factor K (for $K \geq 2/3$ V) is by the methods described in the previous section. For $K < 2/3$ V, consult the data sheet (see Appendix).

The output is given by equation (7-16):

$$e_o = e_{ref}10 - e_i/K + e_{io} \quad (-2 \leq e_i/K \leq +2) \quad \textbf{(7-16)}$$

where e_{io} is the input offset voltage. The procedure for trimming e_{io} in the 759N antilog mode is shown in Fig.

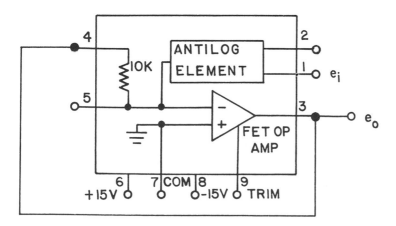

Fig. 7-8. Antilog operation of the Model 759 (reprinted with permission of Analog Devices, Inc.).

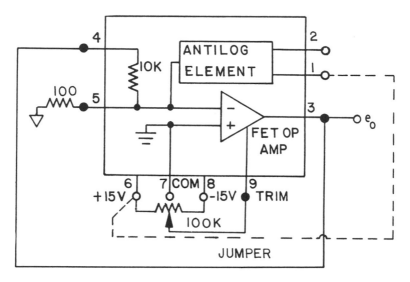

Fig. 7-9. Trimming with the Model 759N in the antilog mode (reprinted with permission of Analog Devices, Inc.).

7-9. The 100 kΩ potentiometer is adjusted for the desired null, with $e_{io} = e_o/100$. After trimming, turn the power off before disconnecting the jumper and 100-ohm resistor. The method for adjusting e_{io} in the 759P is the same as that above, except that the jumper is connected to the − 15 V supply.

To change e_{ref} in the antilog mode, simply disconnect pin 4 from pin 3, and add a resistor between pin 5 and pin 3. The value of the resistor determines the value of e_{ref}, in accordance with equation (7-17).

$$R = \frac{e_{ref}}{10^{-5}A} \qquad (7\text{-}17)$$

In the antilog mode, the 759N produces a positive output and the 759P produces a negative output. Since the maximum output allowed is ± 10 V, e_i/K must not exceed ± 2 V. According to equation (7-16), if e_i/K is greater than ± 2 V, the output e_o exceeds ± 10 V.

PACKAGING THE LOG-ANTILOG MODULE

Since the models 755 and 759 are almost self con-

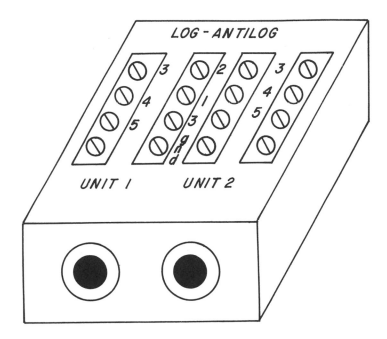

Fig. 7-10. Packaging the log-antilog modules.

tained, packaging them for field use is very simple. All that is needed is the module, a ten-turn 100 kΩ potentiometer, some terminal strips and a box. The module is best mounted on perf board, since its pins are not spaced like those in standard DIP packages.

Since the modules are fairly small, two easily fit in a single box. An example is shown in Fig. 7-10. Again, power supply connections are at the back of the box.

GENERATION OF SINE AND COSINE FUNCTIONS

There are times when it is desirable to obtain both the sine and the cosine of a variable. These two functions are identical except for a phase shift of 90°. A circuit which produces the sine and cosine functions simultaneously is called a *quadrature oscillator* and is quite easy to build, because of the relationship between the two functions.

The general principle behind the quadrature oscillator is shown in Fig. 7-11. If we have a sine wave e_{o1} and feed it into an inverting amplifier (A3), the output is $-A\sin(t/RC)$. If this is then fed into an integrator (A1), the output becomes

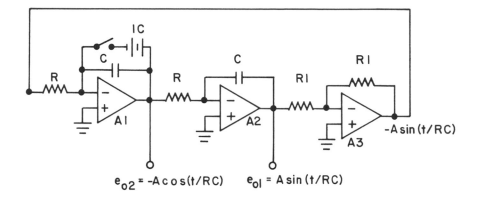

Fig. 7-11. Quadrature oscillator.

$$e_{o2} = -\frac{1}{RC} \int (-Asin(t/RC))dt = -Acos(t/RC) \quad \textbf{(7-18)}$$

since

$$\int sin(pt)dt = -\frac{1}{P}\cos(pt) \quad \textbf{(7-19)}$$

If this output is then fed into another integrator (A2), the output e_{o1} becomes

$$e_{o1} = -\frac{1}{RC} \int \left[-Acos(t/RC)\right]dt = Asin(t/RC) \quad \textbf{(7-20)}$$

since

$$\int cos(pt)dt = \frac{1}{P}\sin(pt) \quad \textbf{(7-21)}$$

This was our starting point. By using two integrators and one inverting amplifier, we are able to produce sine and cosine functions simultaneously.

The frequency of oscillation f of the circuit in Fig. 7-11 is given by equation (7-22):

$$f = \frac{1}{2\pi RC} \quad \textbf{(7-22)}$$

The initial condition applied to A1 sets the value of A.

75

As with the log-antilog generator, a relatively inexpensive precision quadrature oscillator can be purchased in module form. It is the 4423 from Burr-Brown (International Airport Industrial Park, P.O. Box 11400, Tucson, Arizona 85734 (602) 746-1111). The data sheet for the 4423 is reproduced in the Appendix. The circuitry in the 4423 is shown schematically in Fig. 7-12.

Amplifier A3 is an integrator, the output of which is the cosine function (pin 7). The diode network around A3 is a nonlinear amplitude-limiting network. Without it, oscillations would continue to increase in magnitude until the amplifier was saturated. This increases distortion. The diodes clip the output at a level below the saturation limit, thus stabilizing the oscillation. The resistor network around A3 allows the initial condition to be applied.

Amplifier A1 is another integrator, which produces the sine output (pin 1). A2 is an inverting amplifier, and A4 is an uncommitted amplifier contained in the 14-pin DIP package. It can be used as a buffer, level shifter or independent op amp.

The frequency range of the 4423 is from 0.002 Hz to 21.0 kHz. The frequency can be programmed in three ways. First, without any external components, the oscillator produces a sine and cosine output at 20 kHz. This is shown in Fig. 7-13. Second, to program the 4423 for frequencies in the 2 kHz to 20 kHz range, two identical resistors are added, as shown in Fig. 7-14. The value of R for a given frequency is determined by equation (7-23):

$$R = \frac{3.785f}{42.05 - 2f} \quad ; R \text{ in k}\Omega, f \text{ in kHz.} \qquad \textbf{(7-23)}$$

Third, to obtain frequencies down to 0.002 Hz, two equal resistors and two equal capacitors are used, as shown in Fig. 7-15. The frequency is given by equation (7-24):

$$f = \frac{42.05R}{(C + 0.001)(3.785 + 2R)} \qquad \textbf{(7-24)}$$

where f is in Hz, C is in microfarads and R is in kilohms. For best results, the capacitor values should be selected according to frequency range (using Table 7-2). After selecting the capacitor, the resistance is obtained by equation (7-25):

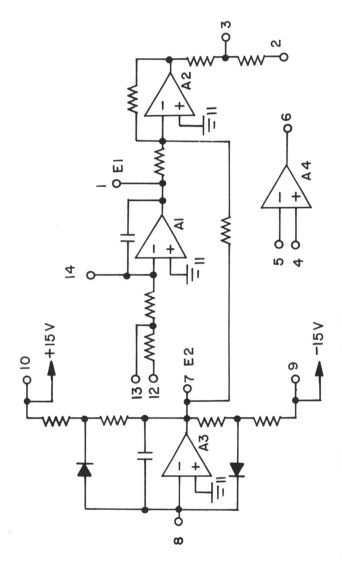

Fig. 7-12. The 4423 quadrature oscillator (courtesy of Burr-Brown).

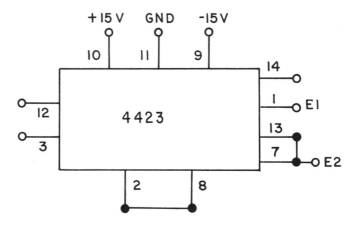

$E1 = 10 \sin 2\pi (20k) t$

$E2 = 10 \cos 2\pi (20k) t$

Fig. 7-13. 20 kHz quadrature (courtesy of Burr-Brown).

$$R = \frac{3.785 f(C + 0.001)}{42.05 - 2f(C + 0.001)} \qquad \textbf{(7-25)}$$

where R is in kilohms, *f* is in Hz and C is in microfarads. As with the integrator, the quadrature requires low-leakage polystyrene, Teflon or polypropylene capacitors.

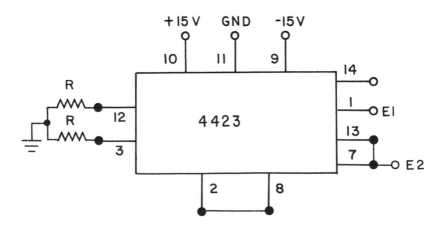

$E1 = 10 \sin 2\pi f t$

$E2 = 10 \cos 2\pi f t$

Fig. 7-14. 2 kHz to 20 kHz quadrature (courtesy of Burr-Brown).

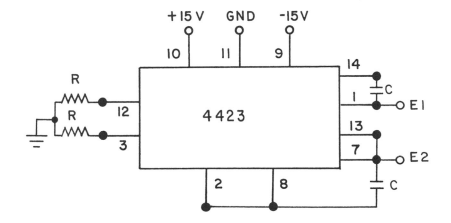

$$E1 = 10 \sin 2\pi f t$$

$$E2 = 10 \cos 2\pi f t$$

Fig. 7-15. Low frequency quadrature (courtesy of Burr-Brown).

At low frequencies, the amplitude of the sine or co-sine wave takes considerable time to build to its peak value (e.g., 250 seconds at 1 Hz). The higher the frequency, the shorter the time necessary to reach peak amplitude (e.g., 0.040 second at 10 kHz). If the quadrature is to be used at very low frequencies, the data sheet should be consulted for advice on how to shorten the amplitude build-up time.

As with the integrator, the quadrature should be activated by a relay. Connection of a DPDT submini 5 Vdc relay (Radio Shack 275-215) in both power supply lines will accomplish this. When the relay power supply is turned on, the quadrature begins oscillating at the same time that integration begins.

The 4423 should be mounted on perf board or universal IC board with the relay. Power supply connections are at the back of the cabinet. As with the log-

Table 7-2. Guide for Capacitor Values (Courtesy of Burr-Brown).

	0.02 Hz	0.2 Hz	2 Hz	20 Hz	200 Hz	2 kHz	20 kHz
	to	to	to	to	to	to	to
f	0.002 Hz	0.02 Hz	0.2 Hz	2 Hz	20 Hz	200 Hz	2 kHz
C	1000 μF	100 μF	10 μF	1 μF	0.1 μF	0.01 μF	0

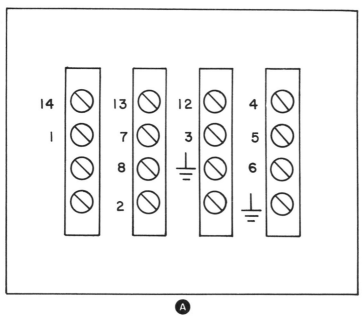

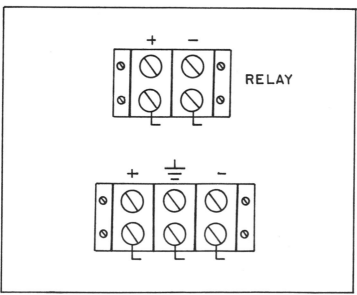

Fig. 7-16. (A) Physical appearance of quadrature module (B) rear view.

antilog generator, external connections are made with terminal strips. The physical appearance of the quadrature is shown in Fig. 7-16.

Chapter 8

Applications

C ONGRATULATIONS! IF YOU HAVE CONSTRUCTED ALL THE CIR-
cuits described in Chapters 2 through 7, you have
the components of a very flexible electronic analog computer. It is time to learn how to use that computer.

There are three specific applications to be discussed
in this chapter. First, we will examine how to solve
differential equations. Second, we will examine how to
generate functions not covered in Chapter 7 through a
process known as *implicit generation*. And third, we will
explore how to use the components of the EAC in process
measurement and control situations.

A word of caution is in order. It is not the purpose
of this chapter to teach you how to solve differential
equations. There are many fine texts available, and these
are generally used in a one semester freshman- or
sophomore-year college differential equations course. To
attempt to condense that much information into a single chapter would be futile. Rather, it is the purpose of
this chapter to acquaint one familiar with differential
equations with the benefits of solutions with the EAC.
This is particularly true with nonlinear differential
equations.

It should also be pointed out that there are several
texts which deal *entirely* with programming the EAC.

These texts are listed in the bibliography. Although they are somewhat dated, the principles espoused in these texts are as valid today as when these books were written.

Having defined the limits of this chapter, we now examine the solution of differential equations.

SOLVING DIFFERENTIAL EQUATIONS

The best way to understand the use of the EAC in problem solving is through examples. In the examples that follow, we will examine first-order differential equations, second-order differential equations, nonlinear differential equations, and simultaneous equations. In the course of working the examples, we will also comment upon amplitude and time scaling, and output devices.

First-Order Differential Equations

First-order differential equations are easy to solve because they involve only one integration. An example is equation (8-1)

$$\frac{dy}{dt\,dt} + ay = 0 \qquad \text{(8-1)}$$

with initial conditions $y = 10$ at $t = 0$. This equation has the solution

$$y = y_o e^{-at} \qquad \text{(8-2)}$$

where y_o is the value of y at $t = 0$, and e is the base of natural logarithms ($e = 2.718281828$). Thus we will be able to compare our computer solution with the known solution.

To begin solving equation (8-1), we rewrite it as shown in equation (8-3).

$$\frac{dy}{dt} = -ay \qquad \text{(8-3)}$$

In other words, the derivative of y is equal to the negative of y scaled by a factor a. This is represented by the computer solution of Fig. 8-1.

The input to the integrator is dy/dt; the output from

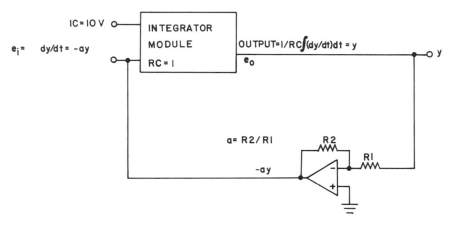

Fig. 8-1. Solution of Equation (8-1).

the integrator is y. The input to the integrator also happens to be – ay, so if we take the integrator's output and scale it by – a (the inverting amplifier with R2/R1 = a), we have the input to the integrator and thus close the feedback loop.

We could also solve equation (8-1) with the circuit of Fig. 8-2. In this case, RC sets 1/a and we use the – e_o terminal of the integrator.

The output of Fig. 8-1 for y_o = 10 and a = 1 is shown in Fig. 8-3, as recorded on a strip chart recorder with 10 volts full scale sensitivity and a chart speed of 0.2 inches/second. Note that the solution falls exponen-

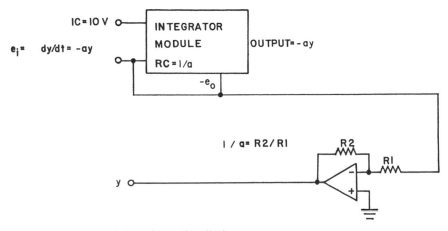

Fig. 8-2. Alternate solution of equation (8-1).

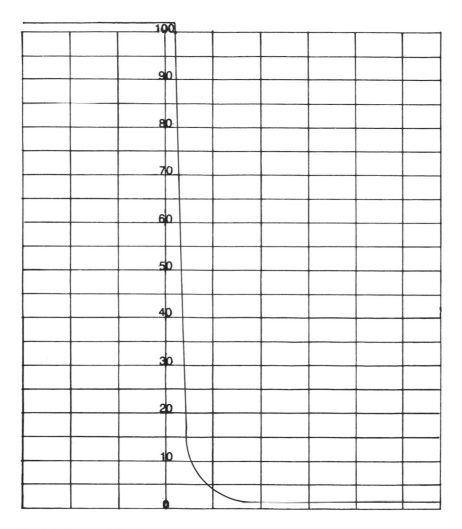

Fig. 8-3. Output of Fig. 8-1.

tially to zero, as predicted by equation 8-2. Since the fastest speed I can obtain on my recorder is 0.2 inches/second, and since the solution is essentially zero after 6 seconds, the whole solution is squeezed into only 1 1/4 inches of chart paper.

In order to spread out the solution, we resort to a technique called *time-scaling*. Let us assume that we want the solution of equation (8-1) to occupy twice as many inches on the chart paper. In other words, we want zero to be reached 2 1/2 inches from the y axis instead of 1 1/4 inches as shown in Fig. 8-3. This amounts to slowing the problem down. That is, we will solve the problem out to six seconds of problem time t, but that will correspond to 12 seconds of EAC computing time T. This is stated mathematically in equation (8-4):

$$t = bT \qquad \textbf{(8-4)}$$

where b is the scaling factor. In this case, $b = 1/2$. Since $b = 1/RC$, we choose $R = 2$ megohms (and $C = 1$ microfarad). The redrawn computer set-up for this problem is given in Fig. 8-4, and the output is given in Fig. 8-5. Notice that the change in variables from t to T is carried out in standard fashion; i.e.,

$$\frac{d^n}{dt^n} = \frac{1}{b^n} \frac{d^n.}{dT^n}$$

It is also worth noting that the time-scaling has no effect on the amplitude of y.

The output of Fig. 8-1 could also be displayed on an oscilloscope. The output voltage is applied to the vertical input of the oscilloscope, while the horizontal sweep is set at a frequency that allows the entire solution to be displayed upon the screen in one sweep. This may require time-scaling. On my oscilloscope, the lowest horizontal sweep rate is 0.2 seconds per centimeter, and the screen is 10 centimeters wide. Thus I can only see 2 seconds of the solution in one sweep. This situation

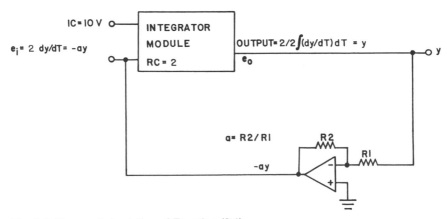

Fig. 8-4. Time-scaled solution of Equation (8-1).

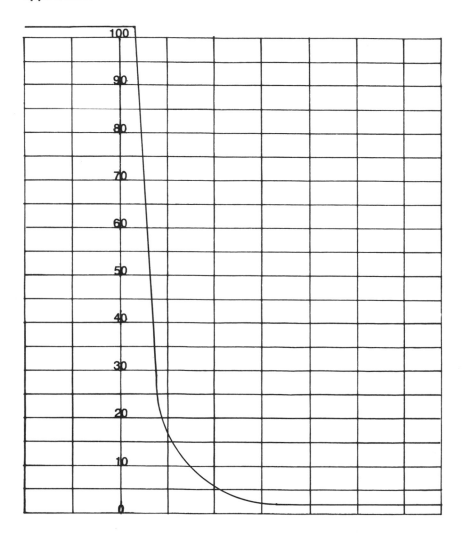

Fig. 8-5. Output of Fig. 8-4.

can be remedied by speeding up the solution with time-scaling. If b in equation (8-4) is set equal to 3, then 6 seconds of problem time can be displayed with only 2 seconds of computing time, and the whole solution can be viewed on an oscilloscope with a 2 seconds-wide screen. The computer set-up for this solution is shown in Fig. 8-6.

The preceding examples of time-scaling show the practical advantages of the technique. In general, equation (8-4) should be used and the rules of changing variables should be followed. To speed up a solution, b

should be greater than 1 (R less than 1). To slow down a solution, b should be less than 1 (R greater than 1). Time-scaling does not affect the amplitude of the y variable.

Aside from the strip chart recorder and oscilloscope, solutions of differential equations can be displayed on X-Y recorders. The X-Y recorder plots two variables: the X (independent) variable (in this case, t) versus the Y (dependent) variable (in this case, y). The sensitivity of each variable can be adjusted independently (e.g., 1 volt/cm, 10 volts/cm, etc.). The output of Fig. 8-1 provides the y input. A linear ramp generator (using an integrator module with a constant input) can be used to feed the X input, as shown in Fig. 8-7. If we wish the X axis to correspond to 1 sec/cm, and the sensitivity of the X channel is one volt/cm, then $RC = 1$ and $e_i = 1$ volt will provide a linear ramp with the proper slope for 10 seconds of integration.

Thus far we have looked at the solution of a first-order differential equation and have examined time-scaling. The three different output devices have been discussed (strip chart recorder, X-Y recorder, oscilloscope). Next we will look at second-order differential equations and the process of amplitude scaling.

Second-Order Differential Equations

Second-order differential equations are only slightly more difficult than first-order equations. They require

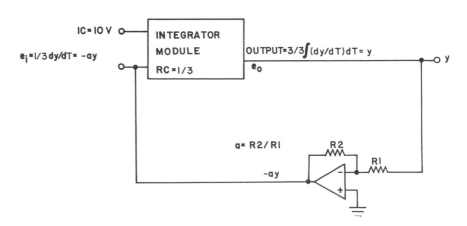

Fig. 8-6. Solution of Equation (8-1) scaled for the oscilloscope.

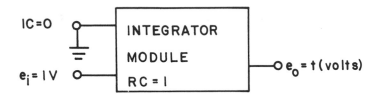

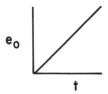

Fig. 8-7. Linear ramp generator.

two integrators (and two initial conditions) instead of one. As an example, let us consider the problem of a ball falling under the influence of gravity.

The height y at any time t of a ball falling under the influence of gravity is given by equation (8-5)

$$\frac{d^2y}{dt^2} = -g \qquad (8\text{-}5)$$

where g is the acceleration due to gravity (32 ft/sec² or 9.8 m/sec²). This equation can be solved by integrating twice. The first integration yields equation (8-6)

$$\frac{dy}{dt} = -gt + \frac{dy}{dt_o} \qquad (8\text{-}6)$$

where dy/dt_o represents the ball's initial velocity. Since the ball was initially at rest, dy/dt_o = 0. Integrating both sides of equation (8-6) yields the solution

$$y = -1/2 \, gt^2 + y_o \qquad (8\text{-}7)$$

where y_o is the height from which the ball is dropped.

The EAC solution for equation (8-5) is shown in Fig. 8-8. In this solution we have assumed that the ball was

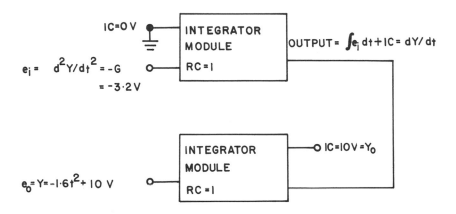

Fig. 8-8. Solution of Equation (8-5).

dropped from a height of 100 feet. Since the op amps saturate at $\pm$ 10 V, we must use *amplitude-scaling* for g and y_o in order to solve the problem. The scale factor we use for y is just equal to 10 V/y_{max}. Since y_{max} = 100 feet, the scale factor is 1/10. Thus,

$$Y = ay \qquad (8\text{-}8)$$

where $a - 0.1$
    Scaling g and y_o follows the same approach. The scale factor for g is also 0.1:

$$G = 0.1g \qquad (8\text{-}9)$$

The scale factor for y_o must be the same as for y:

$$Y_o = 0.1\, y_o \qquad (8\text{-}10)$$

The output from Fig. 8-8 is given by equation (8-11).

$$Y = -\ 1/2\ Gt^2\ +\ Y_o \qquad (8\text{-}11)$$

To convert this to equation (8-7), simply use the relationships in equations (8-8), (8-9), and (8-10).
    The output from Fig. 8-8 is shown in Fig. 8-9. The ball hits the ground (y = 0) at t = 2.5 seconds. Since the strip chart recorder speed is 0.2 inches/second, the

whole solution is recorded on 1/2 inch of chart paper. A more convenient method of recording the solution would be to time-scale so that one inch of chart paper equals one second of time. To do this, we use equation (8-4) with $b = 0.2$ ($R = 5$ megohms). In this way, the solution is slowed down so that 2.5 seconds of problem time t equals 12.5 seconds of computing time T. Since 12.5 seconds × 0.2 inches/second = 2.5 inches of chart paper, the solution is expanded. The computer set-up for this is shown in Fig. 8-10, and its solution is shown in Fig. 8-11.

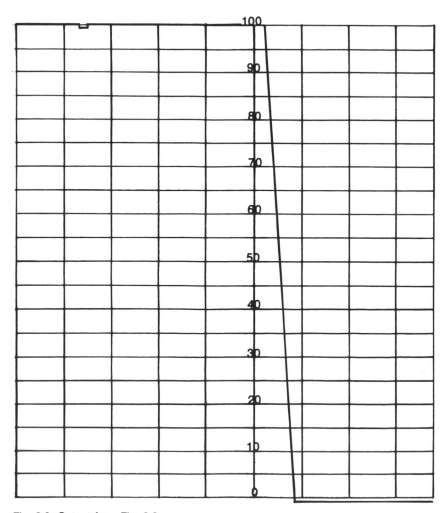

Fig. 8-9. Output from Fig. 8-8.

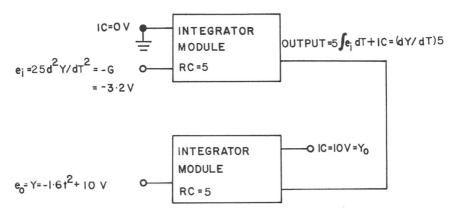

Fig. 8-10. Time-scaled solution of Equation (8-5).

Second-order differential equations occur frequently in physics, chemistry, and the engineering sciences. Some of the more familiar equations, and computer set-ups for their solutions, are given in Fig. 8-12.

Nonlinear Differential Equations

You may have noticed by now that we have been able to solve the preceding differential equations without the EAC. For each equation, both closed-form and computer solutions have been presented. Obviously, if a closed-form solution is attainable, then one does not need to program the EAC.

Closed-form solutions of nonlinear differential equations are rare. Even approximate solutions of nonlinear equations are difficult to obtain. That is why the EAC finds its greatest utility in the solution of nonlinear differential equations.

An example of such an equation is Van der Pol's equation, which describes the buildup of oscillations in a nonlinear electrical system (such as a vacuum-tube oscillator). Van der Pol's equation is given by equation (8-12).

$$\frac{d^2y}{dt^2} - \mu(1 - y^2)\,\frac{dy}{dt} + y = 0 \qquad \textbf{(8-12)}$$

where μ is a constant. This equation is similar to the equation of a damped harmonic oscillator except for the presence of the nonlinear damping term $\mu y^2 dy/dt$, which affects the amplitude of the oscillation. An *approximate* solution of equation (8-12) is given by equation (8-13).

$$y \cong 2 - \left(\frac{29\mu^2}{96w_o^2}\right) \sin(w_o t) + \frac{\mu}{4w_o} \left[\cos(w_o t)\right.$$

(8-13)

$$\left. - \cos(3w_o t)\right] + \frac{\mu^2}{16w_o} \left[3\sin(3w_o t) - \frac{5}{6} \sin(5w_o t)\right]$$

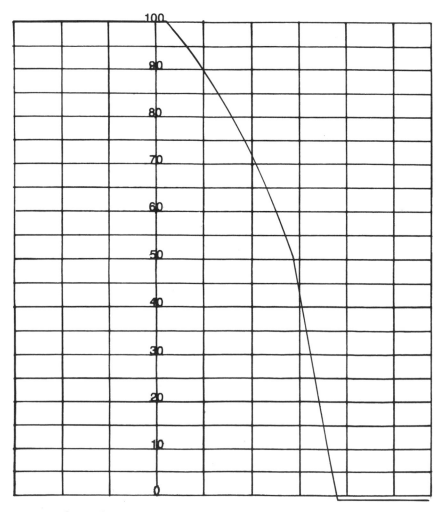

Fig. 8-11. Output from Fig. 8-10.

where $w_o^2 = 1 - \mu^2/8$. As you can see, even an approximate analytical solution of Van der Pol's equation requires a lot of tedious work.

Solving Van der Pol's equation on the EAC, however, is really very simple. The set-up is shown in Fig. 8-13. If we let the value of μ range between 0 and 1, the initial value of dy/dt equal zero, and the initial value of y range between 0 and 2, then none of the values of y, dy/dt or d^2y/dt^2 will exceed 3 volts, so no amplitude scaling is necessary.

Two solutions of Van der Pol's equation are given in Fig. 8-14. Notice that in addition to plotting y versus t, y is also plotted versus dy/dt. This plot is called the *phase-plane diagram*, and displays some interesting behavior. In nonlinear mechanics, it is usually true that the phase-plane diagram is more informative than the standard plot of y versus t. Behavior of solutions in the vicinity of singular points are often studied in this way. In order to display the phase-plane, an X-Y recorder or oscilloscope must be used. The y output is fed into the X channel of the X-Y recorder (or the horizontal input of the oscilloscope), and the dy/dt value is fed into the Y channel of the recorder (or the vertical input of the oscilloscope).

Simultaneous Equations

Simultaneous equations can be solved by hand using Cramer's rule, or they can be solved with the EAC. Consider equation (8-14), which is a system of two linear equations in two unknowns:

$$ax + by = c$$

$$\text{(8-14)}$$

$$dx + ey = f$$

where the two unknowns are x and y and the coefficients a, b, c, d, e and f are known constants. According to Cramer's rule, the values of x and y are given by equation (8-15).

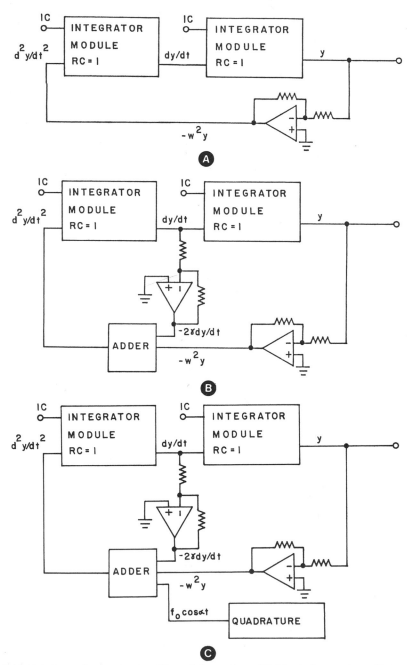

Fig. 8-12. Solutions of second-order differential equations: (A) Simple harmonic oscillator $d^2y/dt^2 + w^2y = 0$ (B) Damped harmonic oscillator $d^2y/dt^2 + 2\gamma dy/dt + w^2y = 0$ (C) Forced oscillator $d^2y/dt^2 + 2\gamma dy/dt + w^2y = f_0 \cos\alpha t$.

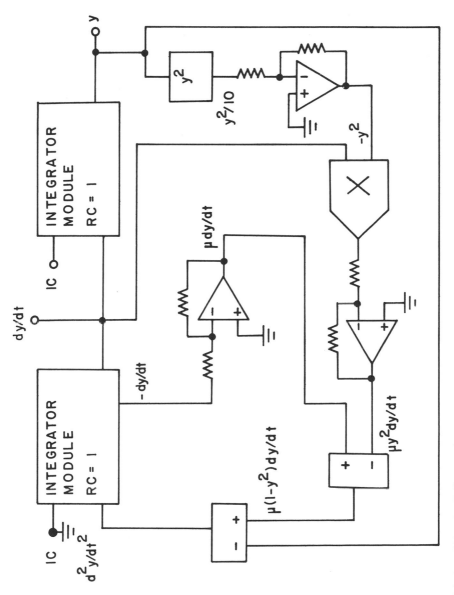

Fig. 8-13. Solution of Van der Pol's equation.

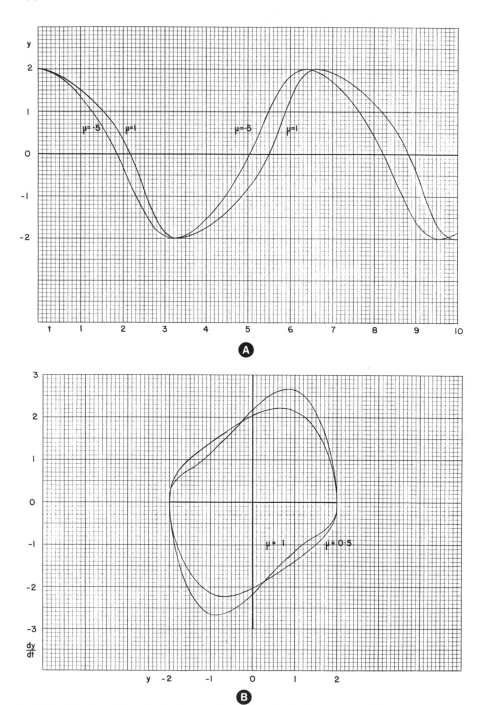

Fig. 8-14. Solution of Van der Pol's equation for initial conditions y = 2, dy/dt = 0 and for two values of μ (μ = 0.5, μ = 1) (A) Plot of y versus t (B) Phase plane plot.

$$x = \cfrac{\begin{vmatrix} c & b \\ f & e \end{vmatrix}}{\begin{vmatrix} a & b \\ d & e \end{vmatrix}} \;,\qquad y = \cfrac{\begin{vmatrix} a & c \\ d & f \end{vmatrix}}{\begin{vmatrix} a & b \\ d & e \end{vmatrix}} \qquad \text{(8-15)}$$

Expanding the determinants in equation (8-15) results in the more explicit solution:

$$x = \frac{ce - fb}{ae - db} \;,\; y = \frac{af - dc}{ae - db} \qquad \text{(8-16)}$$

As you can see, solving systems of linear equations this way becomes very messy as the number of unknowns (and equations) increases.

The solution of equation (8-14) with the EAC is shown in Fig. 8-15. The solution becomes clear when equation (8-14) is rewritten as equation (8-17).

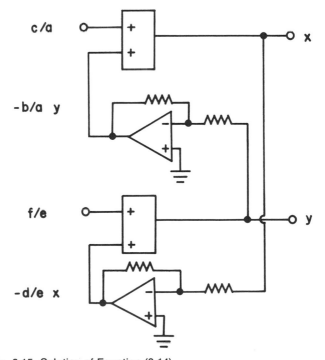

Fig. 8-15. Solution of Equation (8-14).

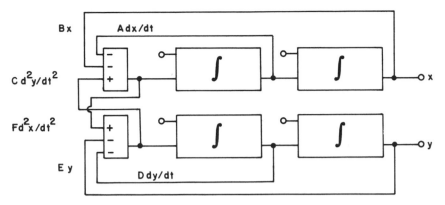

Fig. 8-16. Solution of the system of simultaneous differential equations:

$$d^2x/dt^2 + Adx/dt + Bx - Cd^2y/dt^2 = 0$$
$$d^2y/dt^2 + Ddy/dt + Ey - Fd^2x/dt^2 = 0$$

Coefficients A, B, C, D, E, and F are set by adder/subtractor modules.

$$x = \frac{c}{a} - \frac{b}{a} y \qquad \textbf{(8-17)}$$

$$y = \frac{f}{e} - \frac{d}{e} x$$

The circuit set-up is simple and the solution is obtained very rapidly.

The EAC can be used to solve systems of simultaneous differential equations. An example is shown in Fig. 8-16.

IMPLICIT GENERATION OF FUNCTIONS

The quadrature oscillator of Fig. 7-11 is an example of implicit generation of functions. The equation solved by the circuit of Fig. 7-11 is equation (8-18):

$$\frac{d^2y}{dt^2} + \frac{1}{(RC)^2} y = 0 \qquad \textbf{(8-18)}$$

which has the solution

$$y = A \sin (t/RC) + B \cos (t/RC) \qquad \textbf{(8-19)}$$

When initial conditions of $dy/dt_0 = A$ and $y_0 = 0$ are applied, the $B\cos(t/RC)$ term of equation (8-19) disappears, with the result that the y output is a sine function and the dy/dt output is a cosine function.

Implicit generation of functions simply involves finding a differential equation whose solution is the desired function and solving the equation with the EAC.

Suppose we wish to generate the exponential function $y = y_o e^{-at}$. We could do this with the antilog generator, or we could solve equation (8-1) with the EAC. The output from Fig. 8-1 is the desired function.

Suppose we wish to generate the reciprocal of the above exponential function $y = y_o e^{at}$. The differential equation that has this as its solution is given in equation (8-20)

$$\frac{dy}{dt} - ay = 0 \qquad\qquad \textbf{(8-20)}$$

The computer set-up for the generation of this function is shown in Fig. 8-17.

Hyperbolic sine and cosine functions are generated from equation (8-21)

$$\frac{d^2y}{dt^2} - \frac{1}{(RC)^2} \quad y = 0 \qquad\qquad \textbf{(8-21)}$$

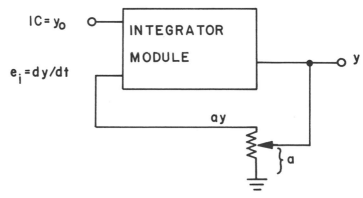

Fig. 8-17. Generation of $y = y_0 e^{at}$.

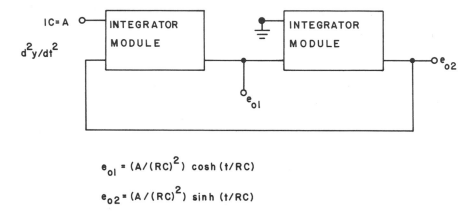

$$e_{o1} = (A/(RC)^2) \cosh(t/RC)$$

$$e_{o2} = (A/(RC)^2) \sinh(t/RC)$$

Fig. 8-18. Generation of hyperbolic functions.

which has as solutions

$$y = A \sinh(t/RC) \text{ and } y = B\cosh(t/RC) \quad \textbf{(8-22)}$$

The choice of initial conditions will determine which of the two above equations is satisfied. Either way, both functions are generated, since one is the derivative of the other (Fig. 8-18).

Many other functions can be generated implicitly. All that is needed is a sound knowledge of differential equations and the appropriate EAC modules.

There is one additional family of functions whose generation will prove useful in solving certain differential equations. This is the family of *powers* of functions. We have constructed a squarer and square rooter in Chapter 5 which will give two powers of functions; i.e., y^2 and $y^{1/2}$. Other powers can be generated with the log-antilog module using equation (8-23)

$$y^n = 10(n\log 10y) \quad \textbf{(8-23)}$$

As an example, let us assume that we want to generate the 5th power of y. Variable y is fed into a log generator, its output is multiplied by 5, and the antilog is taken. This is shown in Fig. 8-19. Roots of variables (i.e., n less than 1) can be generated in the same way.

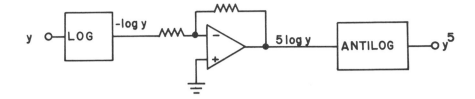

Fig. 8-19. Generation of the fifth power of y.

PROCESS MEASUREMENT
AND CONTROL APPLICATIONS

The area of process measurement and control is too large to be treated properly in just one section. The reader who is interested in a thorough coverage of the topic is referred to the bibliography. In this section we will examine fairly common uses of analog computational circuits in process measurement and control.

In measurement applications, the inputs to the analog computational circuits are no longer provided by a reference voltage source. Instead, the signals are provided by *transducers*, which are devices that convert a measurable quantity into an electrical voltage. Examples of transducers include position transducers (convert length into voltage), strain gauges (convert strains, forces or pressures into electrical resistance, which gives a proportional output voltage), differential pressure cells (convert change in pressure to voltage), thermistors and thermocouples (convert temperature into voltage). Appropriate choices of transducers and computational circuits allow most any physical quantity to be measured.

Let us assume that we want to control the flow rate of a gas in a pipe that leads to a chemical reactor of some sort. In order to control the flow rate, we must first obtain a reliable measurement of flow rate and incorporate that measurement into a feedback loop to the flow controller. The flow rate can be calculated from equation (8-24):

$$\text{Mass Flow Rate} = K \left(\frac{\Delta P \times P_{absolute}}{T_{absolute}} \right)^{1/2} \quad \textbf{(8-24)}$$

where K is a constant. We thus need a differential pressure cell (for ΔP), an absolute pressure transducer, and a temperature transducer calibrated in degrees Kelvin.

101

The circuit for calculating mass flow rate is shown in Fig. 8-20. It incorporates three of the multiplier-divider-squarer-square rooter modules described in Chapter 5. The output can be read directly from a voltmeter and/or fed back to the flow controller.

Another typical use of these circuits is in measuring heat transfer rate. This is given by equation (8-25).

Heat Transfer Rate = C × Flow Rate × ΔT **(8-25)**

The circuit for measuring heat transfer rate is shown in Fig. 8-21.

As a final example, let us consider a chemical reaction that takes place in a sealed vessel. The vessel temperature is controlled, since the reaction becomes explosive at high temperatures. We would like to be able to monitor the vessel temperature and the rate of change in vessel temperature. The circuit for doing this is shown in Fig. 8-22. The output from a temperature transducer is amplified and displayed, so that the temperature is known. Additionally, the output is differentiated, so that the rate of change is known. This signal is fed to an alarm

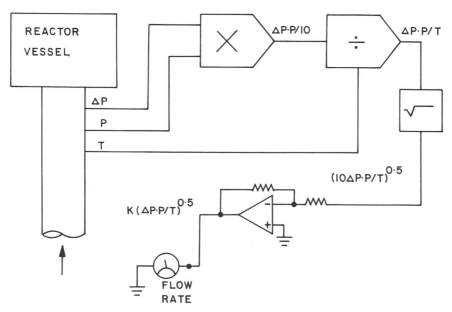

Fig. 8-20. Measurement of mass flow rate.

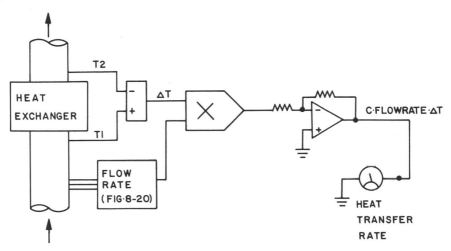

Fig. 8-21. Measurement of heat transfer rate.

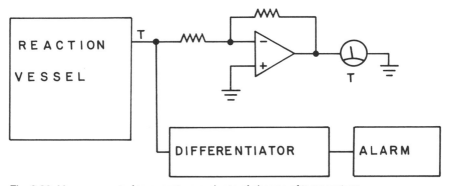

Fig. 8-22. Measurement of temperature and rate of change of temperature.

that is triggered if the rate of change in temperature exceeds a safe limit.

As stated previously, these are but a few examples of the important role analog computational circuits play in industrial applications. For further examples on this subject, the reader is advised to consult the Bibliography.

Chapter 9

Process Control

T HE APPLICATIONS OF ANALOG COMPUTATIONAL CIRCUITS discussed in Chapter 8 covered primarily the solution of differential equations and function generation. Only three examples of process measurement and control were presented. Although analog computational circuits are used to solve equations and generate functions, their principal use today is in the area of process control. In this chapter, we will take a closer look at process control applications.

After examining the behavior of an uncontrolled system, we will study the *proportional control* scheme. The response of the proportionally-controlled system will be compared with responses of systems controlled by refined schemes, such as *proportional-integral* (PI), *proportional-derivative* (PD), and *proportional-integral-derivative* (PID) control. All of these methods will be evaluated for a model system.

This chapter will conclude with several illustrative examples of process control applications. The reader is reminded that this chapter will provide only a general introduction to the area of process control. Those interested in learning more about the area are advised to consult the texts listed in the Bibliography.

THE UNCONTROLLED SYSTEM

The model system to be examined is shown in Fig. 9-1. In this system, a chemical reactor is fed by a reactant stream at a specified temperature T. At a temperature less than T, the yield of product produced by the reactor is diminished so that the reaction becomes uneconomical. At a temperature greater than T, the reaction becomes quite vigorous, eventually approaching an explosive level. Thus, economic and safety considerations require that the reactant stream be maintained at or near temperature T.

The temperature of the reactant stream is controlled by the valve in the cooling water line. When the valve is opened, cooling water flows to the heat exchanger and the reactant stream is cooled down. As the valve is closed, less cooling water is allowed to flow to the heat exchanger, and the temperature of the reactant stream is increased to the ambient level (which is above the safe limit).

In the uncontrolled system of Fig. 9-1, a human operator would be assigned the responsibility of monitoring the temperature and adjusting the cooling water flow rate accordingly. In other words, the operator becomes the *feedback* mechanism. It is likely that the operator has other responsibilities, so that he is not available for continuous measurement and control.

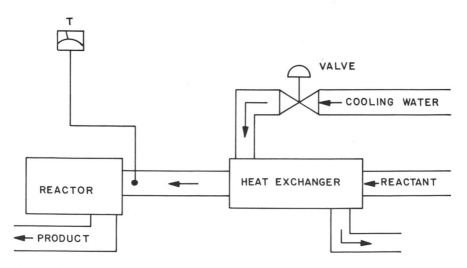

Fig. 9-1. The model system.

TEMPERATURE

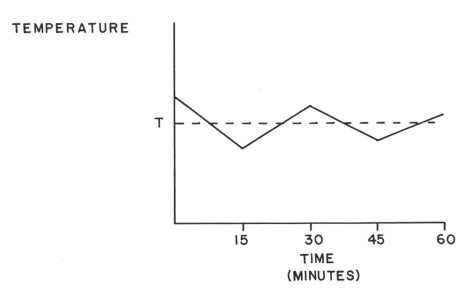

Fig. 9-2. Temperature versus time for an uncontrolled system.

If it is assumed that the operator measures the temperature and adjusts the cooling water flow rate four times an hour, then Fig. 9-2 could represent the temperature versus time plot for the system over the course of an hour. The figure shows that much of the time the temperature of the reactant stream is very different from the desired (or *set point*) temperature T. The reactor spends most of the hour either producing low yields of product or producing reasonable yields under unsafe conditions.

Simple modifications to this system can be made. The temperature signal can be differentiated and fed to an alarm, as was shown in Fig. 8-22, to warn the operator when the rate of change of temperature approaches a dangerous level. The fundamentals of control of such a system, however, would not be different from that of Fig. 9-1.

A sudden upset or step change in reactant stream temperature is shown in Fig. 9-3. If, as shown in the figure, the upset occurs shortly after the operator has adjusted cooling water flow, the result could be disastrous. The temperature could increase to the explosive limit before the next check is made. If the alarm system of Fig. 8-22 is not present, an explosion would very likely occur.

Obviously, the uncontrolled system leaves much to

107

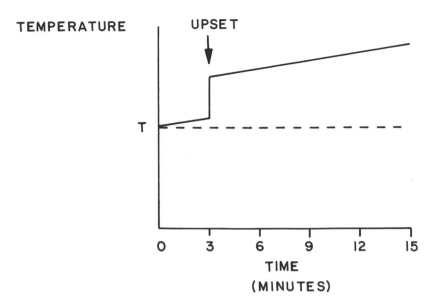

Fig. 9-3. Effect of an upset on an uncontrolled system.

be desired. An improvement over this system is the system with proportional control. This will be discussed in the next section.

PROPORTIONAL CONTROL

The simplest automatic control scheme that could be used on the model system of Fig. 9-1 is the *proportional control* scheme. It is so named because the proportional controller adjusts cooling water flow rate *in proportion* to the amount of error in the temperature reading (i.e., the difference between actual temperature and desired temperature). This is shown in Fig. 9-4.

A comparison of Fig. 9-1 and 9-4 shows the primary differences between the two schemes. First, a device called a proportional controller replaces the human operator as a feedback mechanism. The controller thus provides continuous feedback, whereas the operator provided only intermittent feedback. Second, the proportional controller is fed a temperature set point signal T_s. This signal represents the desired operating temperature. And third, the manual valve adjusted by the operator in Fig. 9-1 has been replaced with an electronic control valve in Fig. 9-4.

The electronic control valve is shown in Fig. 9-5. The valve is opened and closed by a servomechanism that contains a reversible motor. The valve position is controlled by the signal from the proportional controller. In this example, and those that follow, it will be assumed that the valve is opened when a negative control signal is received, and closed when a positive control signal is received. When the input control signal is at zero volts, the valve position is not changed. It will also be assumed that the control valve is linear; i.e., that the valve position varies linearly with the control signal, from a completely opened to a completely closed position. It should be noted that a pneumatic or hydraulic control valve could be used. In fact, these valves are used more often than electronic control valves, partially because they are less expensive. The electronic control valve is used in the example to expedite understanding of the control scheme. The same process control principles that will be applied to the electronic control valve are equally valid for pneumatic or hydraulic control valves.

The proportional control scheme is described mathematically by equation (9-1);

$$e = K\epsilon + e_c \qquad\qquad \textbf{(9-1)}$$

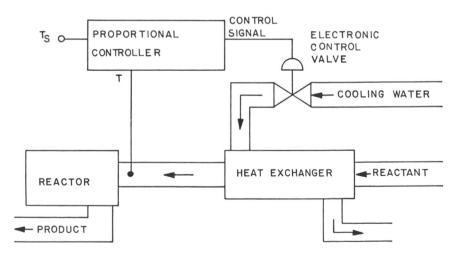

Fig. 9-4. The proportional control scheme.

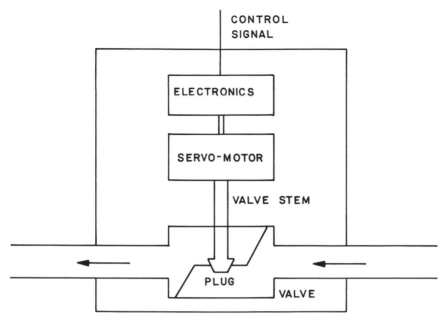

Fig. 9-5. The electronic control valve.

where

> e = voltage output from the controller (i.e., the control signal)
> K = gain
> ϵ = error signal = $T_s - T$
> e_c = a constant
> T_s = set point temperature
> T = measured temperature

From equation (9-1), it can be seen that the control signal e is *proportional* to the error signal ϵ. In fact, equation (9-1) is just the equation for a straight line. Since the electronic control valve in this example does not change position when e is zero volts, the value of the constant e_c will be zero. Thus equation (9-1) becomes

$$e = K \epsilon \qquad (9\text{-}2)$$

Equation (9-2) involves only subtraction ($\epsilon = T_s - T$) and multiplication by a constant coefficient (K). Both of these operations can be performed with the adder/subtractor module described in Chapter 4. Thus the proportional controller is nothing more than a subtractor. This is shown in Fig. 9-6.

The operation of the system is as follows. When the temperature of the reactant stream equals the set point (or desired) temperature (i.e., when the voltage from the thermocouple is the same as the voltage provided by the voltage reference source), the output from the adder/subtractor module is zero. A zero input to the electronic control valve does not alter the valve position, and the flow rate of cooling water to the heat exchanger remains constant. If, however, the reactant stream temperature T is higher than the desired set point, the output from the adder/subtractor module is a negative voltage (since $T > T_s$). A negative value of e causes the servomotor to open the valve and allow more cooling water to flow to the heat exchanger, thus driving T down. When T reaches T_s, the value of e is zero again, and the control valve remains stationary. If, on the other hand, T is less than T_s, a positive e is supplied to the control valve, and the flow of cooling water is reduced.

The value of K depends upon the input parameters of the control valve and the maximum voltage difference between T_s and T. For example, let us assume that the control valve is fully opened when $e = -1$ volt, and fully closed when $e = +1$ volt. Further, let us assume that the reactor approaches the explosive limit when the value of $T_s - T$ is -0.1 volt. Since the valve should be

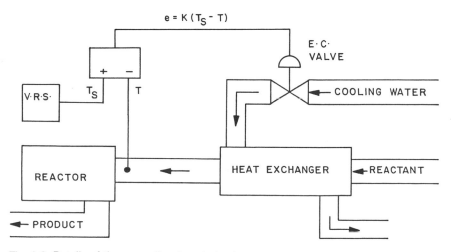

Fig. 9-6. Details of the proportional control scheme.

fully opened at the explosive limit we have from equation (9-2)

$$K = \frac{e}{\epsilon} = \frac{-1}{-0.1} = 10 \qquad (9\text{-}3)$$

The value of K is fixed by the input resistors in the adder/subtractor module (resistors R1 – R8 in Fig. 4-4).

The temperature versus time plot for the proportionally controlled system of Fig. 9-6 is shown in Fig. 9-7, and is compared with a system having no control action. In this figure, it is assumed that the control system is ideal ; i.e., that equation (9-2) is obeyed exactly. It can be seen from the figure that with no control at all the temperature of the reactant stream increases constantly, eventually approaching the explosive limit. With proportional control, however, the temperature oscillates back and forth around the set point temperature, eventually reaching equilibrium there.

The oscillatory approach to the set point temperature is caused by time lags in the system. Control valves do not open instantaneously, and heat exchangers do not drop temperatures immediately. Because of the time lags in valve and heat exchanger operation, it can be seen that the controller overcorrects for temperature; i.e., the

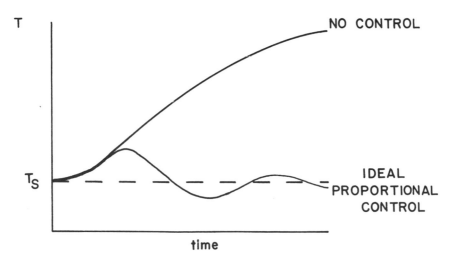

Fig. 9-7. Comparison of ideal proportional control with no control.

controller drives the reactant stream temperature below the set point value. The controller again senses the error and attempts to compensate. Again, the controller overshoots the mark, but not by quite as much as before. This process continues until the reactant stream temperature is very nearly equal to the set point temperature. Thus, the action of the controller, as shown in Fig. 9-7, appears to be that of a damped oscillator.

Figure 9-7 shows the response of an ideal proportional controller to a change in temperature. Figure 9-8 shows the response of a real (i.e., nonideal) proportional controller. As can be seen from the figure, the temperature of the reactant stream reaches a steady-state value higher than that of the set point temperature. The difference between the steady state and set point temperatures is called the *offset*.

This offset occurs because equation (9-2) is not followed exactly. Equation (9-2) is the steady-state control equation. It assumes that the change in temperature from the set-point value occurs instantaneously. This is not usually the case. The effect of the finite time required to make a change in temperature is the addition of a term to equation (9-2), as shown in equation (9-4):

$$e = K\epsilon + f(t,K) \qquad \textbf{(9-4)}$$

where the function $f(t,K)$ is called the *transient response*. The transient response is a function of time and gain, and is largely responsible for the offset.

Another contributor to the offset is the input offset voltage of real op amps. This can become significant, particularly at high gains.

In the model system, an offset cannot be tolerated. A better control scheme must be found. Such a scheme is described in the next section.

PROPORTIONAL-INTEGRAL CONTROL

The offset shown in Fig. 9-8 is due primarily to the transient response, which is a function of gain and time. In order to remove this offset, equation (9-2) must be modified by a term that corrects for the transient response. Such a term is shown in equation (9-5):

$$e = K\epsilon + K/\tau \int_{t=0}^{t} \epsilon \, dt \qquad \textbf{(9-5)}$$

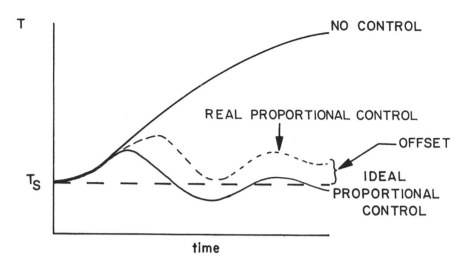

Fig. 9-8. Comparison of real proportional control with ideal proportional control and no control.

where τ is a time constant (set by the values of RC for the integrator-differentiator module described in Chapter 6). Equation (9-5) describes mathematically the *proportional-integral control* scheme.

The control signal e is now proportional to the error and to the time integral of the error. If it is assumed that a unit change in temperature occurs (i.e., that $\epsilon = 1$), the response of the controller becomes:

$$e = K + (K/\tau)t + c \qquad \textbf{(9-6)}$$

where c is a constant, which is determined from initial conditions. Thus with a unit change in temperature, e changes suddenly by an amount equal to K (proportional action), and then changes linearly with time, at a rate equal to K/τ. In this way the offset due to transient response is removed.

In Fig. 9-9 the control action of the proportional-integral controller is compared with that of the proportional controller and no control. The offset in temperature is removed by proportional-integral control, and the steady-state value approaches that of the set point. Proportional-integral control approximates ideal proportional control, with the same degree of oscillatory behavior. Although the offset is removed, it takes a long time for the oscillations about the set point to dampen. This will be discussed further in the next section.

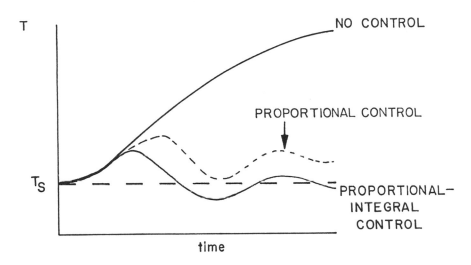

Fig. 9-9. Comparison of no control, proportional control, and proportional-integral control.

The proportional-integral control scheme is shown in Fig. 9-10. The scheme requires one voltage reference source (Chapter 3), one integrator/differentiator module (Chapter 6) and two adder/subtractor modules (Chapter 4).

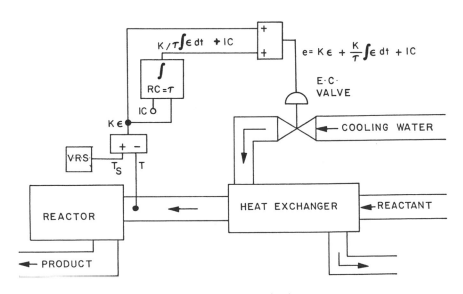

Fig. 9-10. Details of the proportional-integral control scheme.

OSCILLATIONS AND
PROPORTIONAL-DERIVATIVE ACTION

The principal drawback of the proportional-integral control scheme is the oscillatory nature of its response to upsets. On the surface, this appears to be a small price to pay for the benefits of control. From Fig. 9-9 it can be seen that the proportional-integral controller does by far the best job of holding the temperature near the set point. But there are circumstances in which the oscillations of the proportional-integral controller are unacceptable.

It was stated in the previous section that time lags exist between the measurement of temperature and the onset of corrective action. This is due to the fact that mechanical equipment, such as the electronic control valve, do not respond instantaneously to control signals. In other words, a control valve requires a finite amount of time to open after the signal to open has been received. In that interval of time, the measured variable may have changed values. The change in the measured variable can have drastic effects on overall system control.

An example should make this clear. Figure 9-11 represents a system that is uncontrolled; that is, there is no *automatic* control provision. It happens that the temperature of the reactant stream is not constant, but the variations in temperature are regular. This oscillation about the set-point temperature is not terribly inconvenient; however, the product yield from the reaction could be improved if the reactant temperature were held constant. The decision is made to install proportional-integral control.

It just happens that the equipment available for installation has a very large time lag built in it, as shown in Fig. 9-12. The lag is exactly one cycle. At the time of measurement shown in the figure, the temperature is at its highest, and the signal sent to the control valve is nearly a maximum. The control valve does not open to near maximum until one cycle later, at which time the temperature is still at a maximum. Although the time lag is severe, the phase difference reinforces the proper control action, and the cooling water flows to the heat exchanger when temperature is high. The output from the controller, shown in Fig. 9-13, is oscillatory, but is an improvement over no control.

Let us now assume that the PI system has been so successful that the plant manager authorizes the money

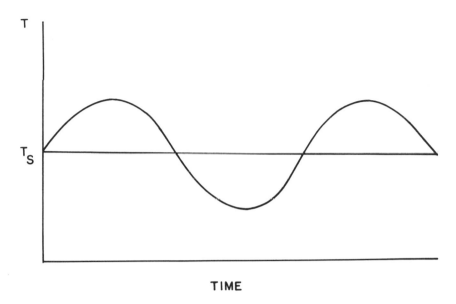

Fig. 9-11. Uncontrolled system with sinusoidal variation in reactant temperature.

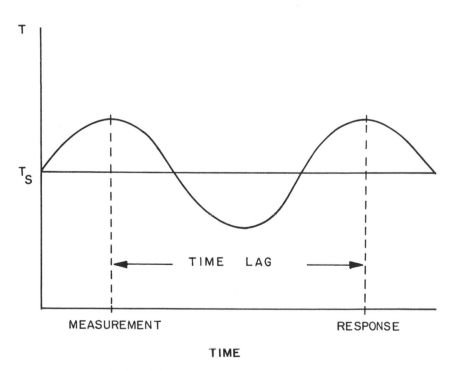

Fig. 9-12. One cycle time lag.

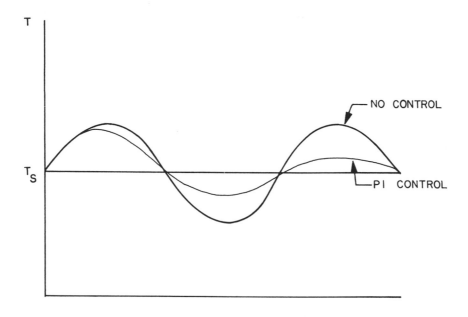

TIME

Fig. 9-13. Proportional-integral system response for a one cycle time lag.

necessary to purchase new equipment. This new equipment has a one-half cycle time lag, which is quite an improvement over the old system. Will its performance be better than that of the old system?

Probably not. This is shown in Fig. 9-14. When the temperature is at a maximum, the signal is sent to the control valve to open. Unfortunately the action is completed when the reactant stream temperature is at a minimum. This phase difference interferes with proper control action, and actually drives the system in the wrong direction. The electrical analog of this is positive feedback, which causes oscillations. From Fig. 9-15 it can be seen that instead of behaving as a damped oscillator, the output from the proportional-integral controller behaves as a self-amplified oscillator. The oscillations feed upon themselves and the amplitude of the oscillations increase. The consequences of such a control scheme are disastrous.

The *phase* of the feedback in a control system is important for stability, just as the phase of the feedback in an amplifier is important. When the phase of the feed-

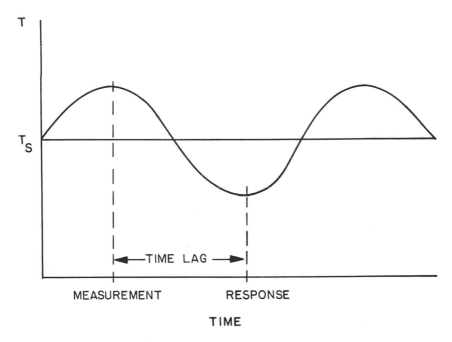

Fig. 9-14. One-half cycle time lag.

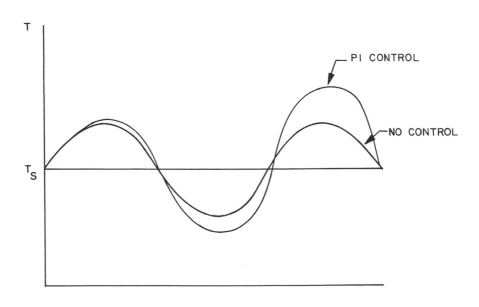

Fig. 9-15. Proportional-integral system response for a one-half cycle time lag.

back in an amplifier is incorrect, the amplifier oscillates: the same was found to be true in the preceding controller example. If we carry this analogy one step further, we will find another variable that is important for controller stability: the controller gain, K.

High-gain amplifiers are more likely to oscillate than low-gain amplifiers. For many of the same reasons, high gains in process control equipment make the equipment more susceptible to oscillation, such as was shown in Fig. 9-15. Since the gain K of the proportional or proportional-integral controller is fixed by the output voltage level of the thermocouple and the input voltage levels required by the electronic control valve, there is little that can be done with this variable to minimize the potential for oscillation.

It is fortunate that, in most applications, the variation in the controlled variable is not as periodic and regular as that shown in Fig. 9-11. Also, advances in component and transducer technology have allowed a general reduction in K values and time lags. Nevertheless, the potential for self-amplified oscillation exists whenever there is an oscillation in the controlled variable. In spite of the fact that proportional-integral control is an improvement over proportional control, it is not good enough for many applications.

What is needed is a method of *anticipating* the change in the controlled variable. With such a method, the present error could be corrected, and the trend in the controlled variable would be discernable. With that trend in view, corrective steps could be taken without resorting to sudden changes that are too late to be effective, and which tend to throw high gain, oscillatory systems into self-amplified oscillation.

Perhaps such a method of anticipating changes in the controlled variable can be found. Consider Fig. 9-16. The curve in the figure represents a sinusoidally-varying variable, such as T. At point 1, the value of the variable is zero. However, the *slope* at point 1 is 1. At point 2, the variable has the value 0.707, and, coincidentally, so does the slope. At point 3, the variable has the value of 1, while the slope at point 3 is zero. Table 9-1 gives a listing of the variable and its slope for all nine points.

From the table it can be seen that the slope anticipates the value of the variable by one-fourth cycle. In other words, the value of the variable at point 3 is anticipated by the slope at point 1, just as the value of the

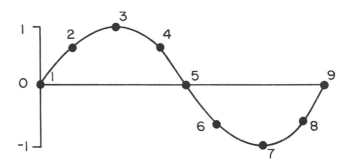

Fig. 9-16. Sinusoidal variation.

variable at point 4 is anticipated by the slope at point 2. The slope, then, appears to be a candidate for removing the oscillations found in proportional or proportional-integral control.

Mathematically, the slope of a function is given by the *derivative* of that function (see Chapter 6). With this in mind, we are led to the *proportional-derivative* control scheme. This scheme is described mathematically by equation (9-6):

$$e = K\epsilon + K\tau d\epsilon/dt \qquad (9\text{-}6)$$

where τ is a time constant (set by the values of RC for the integrator-differentiator module described in Chapter 6).

The control signal e is now proportional to the error signal ($K\epsilon$) and to the derivative of the error signal ($K\tau d\epsilon/dt$). The first term corrects for the difference between T and T_s, while the second term adds to the signal an amount that *anticipates* the change in T.

The control action of the proportional-derivative controller is shown in Fig. 9-17, and is compared with the output of the proportional controller and no control.

As with proportional control, the proportional-

Table 9-1. The Variable and Slope for the Nine Points in Fig. 9-16.

Point	1	2	3	4	5	6	7	8	9
Variable	0	.707	1	.707	0	−.707	−1	−.707	0
Slope	1	.707	0	−.707	−1	−.707	0	.707	1

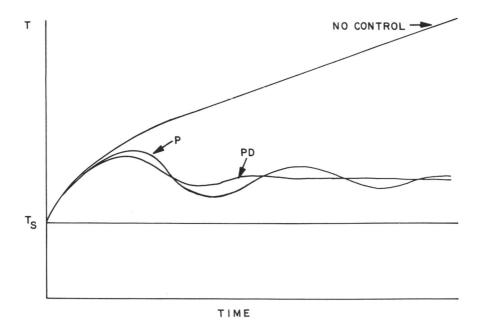

Fig. 9-17. Comparison of proportional and proportional-derivative control with no control.

derivative controller suffers from an offset. The remedy for that is integral action, and this will be considered in the next section. Notice, however, that the oscillations associated with proportional control are quickly damped with proportional-derivative control.

Details of the proportional-derivative control scheme are given in Fig. 9-18. The necessary equipment includes a voltage reference source for the set point (Chapter 3), two adder/subtractor modules (Chapter 4), and one integrator-differentiator module (Chapter 6).

THE PROPORTIONAL-
INTEGRAL-DERIVATIVE (PID) CONTROLLER

Combining the proportional-integral and proportional-derivative controllers yields the *proportional-integral-derivative* (PID) controller. This scheme has the advantages of both systems. The PI action removes offset, and the PD action eliminates excessive oscillation. The output of the PID controller is shown in Fig. 9-19 in comparison with all the other control schemes.

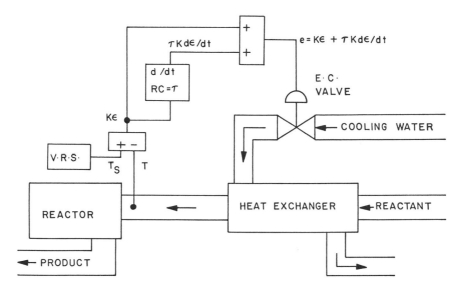

Fig. 9-18. Details of the proportional-derivative control scheme.

The details of the PID controller are shown in Fig. 9-20. It requires a voltage reference source (Chapter 3), two adder/subtractor modules (Chapter 4), and two

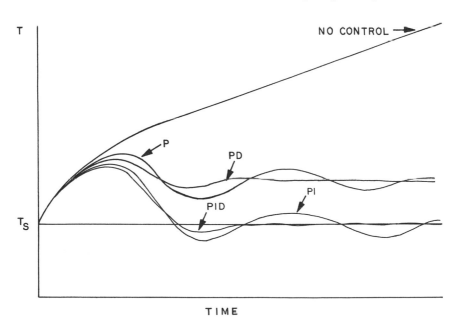

Fig. 9-19. Comparison of the proportional-integral-derivative control scheme with all others.

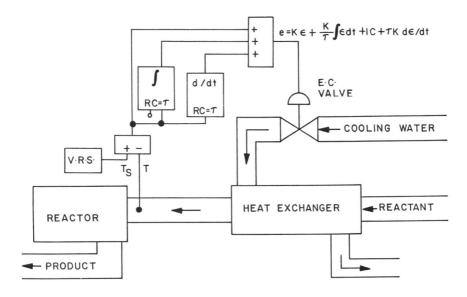

Fig. 9-20. Details of the proportional-integral-derivative control scheme.

integrator-differentiator modules (Chapter 6). It follows equation (9-7):

$$e = K\epsilon + \frac{K}{\tau} \int_{t=0}^{t} \epsilon dt + K\tau d\epsilon/dt \qquad \textbf{(9-7)}$$

APPLICATIONS OF PROCESS CONTROL

Process control is widely used in nearly every industry. Almost any process can benefit from automatic control. Even a control scheme as simple as proportional control is capable of improving the operation of a process.

Consider, for example, a batch reactor that produces a prescription drug. The yield of the reactor (i.e., the amount of product actually produced compared to the amount of product theoretically possible) determines whether or not the reactor is profitable. If it is assumed that the yield varies with temperature, then there should be a temperature range over which the reactor is profitable. If the temperature falls outside that range, the reactor is not producing sufficient product to cover the costs of raw materials, energy, labor, etc. This is shown in Fig. 9-21. Operation within the lined region is profitable.

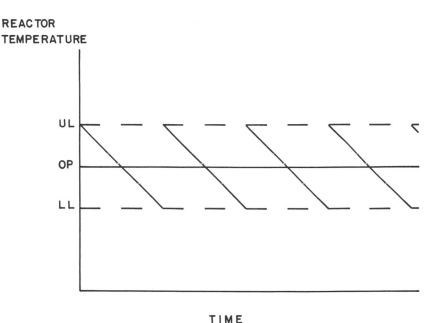

REACTOR
TEMPERATURE

UL

OP

LL

TIME

Fig. 9-21. Profitable temperature range for a reactor. UL stands for upper temperature limit for profitability, LL stands for lower temperature limit for profitability, and OP stands for optimum temperature.

Normal temperature fluctuations within the reactor often fall outside the profitable range. As shown in Fig. 9-22, an uncontrolled reactor could spend as much as 50% of its reaction time outside the limits of profitability. Proportional control, which suffers from oscillatory behavior and an offset, has the potential of improving the reactor's profitability simply because it holds the temperature more or less constant within the profitable region (Fig. 9-23). And the cost of proportional control is minimal, as it involves only a voltage reference source and an adder/subtractor module.

Of course, process control applications are not restricted to the manufacturing industries. There are many examples to be found in your house or apartment. The wall thermostat is one good example. The set point temperature is dialed in, and the room temperature is measured. Whenever the thermostat senses a difference between the two, a feedback control signal is sent to the furnace (or air conditioner). The control signal continues until the room temperature and set-point temperature are equal (or until the difference between the two is equal to a constant offset).

125

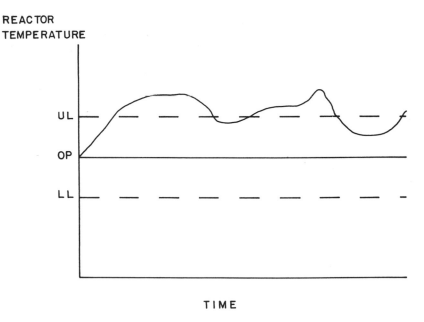

Fig. 9-22. Temperature variation of an uncontrolled reactor.

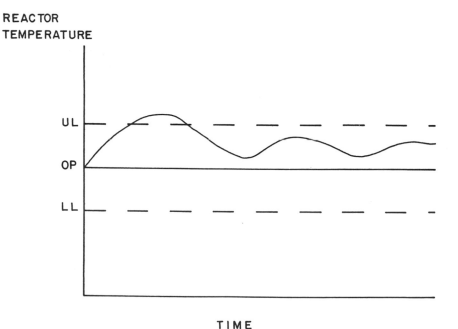

Fig. 9-23. Temperature variation of reactor with proportional control. Time spent outside the profitable region has been greatly reduced.

In this section, several examples of process control applications will be given. These examples are not exhaustive, nor are they particularly complex. They are designed to illustrate the flexibility of the analog computational circuits presented in this book. As with other sections of this book, further details can be found by consulting the references listed in the Bibliography.

Steam Temperature Control

Most industries use steam in one capacity or another. The many uses of steam include power generation and drying. The temperature of the steam depends upon its degree of saturation. Unsaturated steam (dry steam or superheated steam) has the highest temperature, while saturated steam (wet steam or desuperheated steam) has the lowest temperature. For example, saturated steam at an absolute pressure of 150 pounds per square inch has a temperature of 358.42 °F. As moisture is removed from the steam, at the same pressure, its temperature increases. It is not impossible to obtain 150 psi steam at a temperature of 1600 °F!

High temperatures accelerate corrosion, and for that reason it is often desirable to reduce the steam temperature. In this example, a proportional control scheme for the control of steam temperature will be shown.

The system is given schematically in Fig. 9-24. The

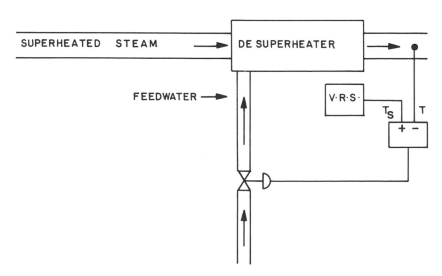

Fig. 9-24. Proportional control of steam temperature.

temperature of the steam is controlled by a device called a desuperheater. Desuperheating occurs when water is sprayed into the steam, which increases its moisture content (up to saturation) and lowers the temperature. The control signal will therefore open or close the feedwater control valve. Temperature is measured on the downstream side of the desuperheater, compared with the set point (from the voltage reference source), and the difference signal (from the adder/subtractor module) is fed to the control valve.

The thermodynamics of steam are such that wild oscillations are not a problem. Thus the only real difficulty with proportional control in this application is the offset. In this case offset can be corrected very easily. The temperature set point is simply lowered by the amount of the offset. For example, if the proportional controller has a constant offset of twenty percent, the temperature set point can be lowered by twenty percent.

Consistency Control

Most refineries, chemical manufacturing plants, pharmaceutical plants and paper mills are criss-crossed with pipes and filled with pumps. The most convenient method of moving raw materials or products back and forth in a plant is by pumping. When the material to be moved is a liquid, there are usually no problems using pumps. Generally, however, dry materials cannot be pumped.

If, however, the dry materials are first slurried (i.e., mixed with water), then they can be pumped. This is a common method of pumping pigments such as clay. Such a slurry is characterized by its *consistency*, which is just the percentage of dry material in the slurry. A pump is then selected that can handle the desired consistency.

Consistency control is important for two reasons. First, if consistency becomes too great, the pump will not be capable of moving the slurry. And second, the proper mixing of slurries for particular applications will depend upon the availability of a constant concentration of dry material in the slurry. Thus, consistency control is often a critical requirement.

The first step in devising a consistency control scheme is the selection of a consistency measuring device. Such a device is shown in Fig. 9-25. The slurry

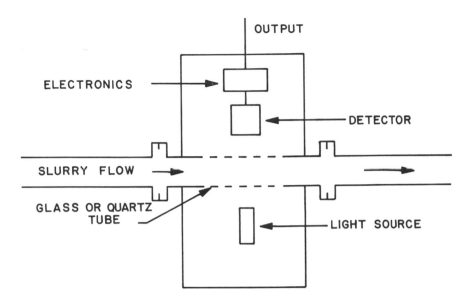

Fig. 9-25. Device for the measurement of consistency.

passes through a clear glass or quartz tube, through which light is transmitted. As the consistency of the slurry is increased, the light received by the detector is decreased (that is, the slurry becomes more opaque); when the consistency of the slurry is decreased, the light received is increased (the slurry becomes more transparent). The detector signal is then treated by the electronics package within the measurement device and boosted to the appropriate level. The consistency measuring device can be calibrated with slurries prepared in a laboratory at known consistencies. In general, the calibration would be different for different materials, such as clay, calcium carbonate, wood pulp, etc.

The control scheme for a simple, one-step dilution is shown in Fig. 9-26. The consistency measuring device is located on the outlet side of the pump. The reason for this is that the pump is the only mixing element in this system, and the slurry should be well mixed before measuring consistency. The consistency signal is then compared with the set point signal (from the voltage reference source), and the control signal is then fed back to the electronic control valve in the dilution water line. If consistency is too high, dilution water flow is increased, and if consistency is too low, dilution wa-

129

ter flow is decreased. In this example, proportional control is used.

The system of Fig. 9-26 works best when small changes in consistency are required. If large dilution water flow rates are required, consistency control becomes erratic. This can be remedied with the two-step dilution system shown in Fig. 9-27.

In the two-step system, the secondary dilution control step is just the same as before. What is new is a primary dilution step in which the dilution water is mixed with the slurry in an agitated tank. When the consistency error signal is large, such that the secondary control valve is almost fully opened, a second proportional controller increases primary dilution water flow. Thus the primary dilution system acts as a gross adjustment to consistency, while the secondary dilution system fine-tunes the flow to the desired consistency.

Level Control

In the previous example, a tank was employed in the primary dilution system. Tanks find many applications in the process industries. They are used as reservoirs, as mixing elements and as buffers. In working with tanks, however, care must be taken to assure that they are neither drawn down nor overfilled. The amount of

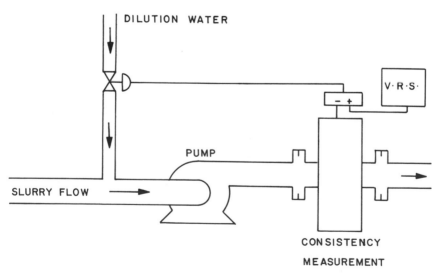

Fig. 9-26. Proportional control of consistency for a one-step dilution.

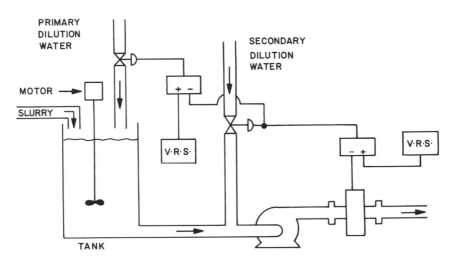

Fig. 9-27. Proportional control of consistency for a two-step dilution.

mixture leaving a tank should just equal the amount of liquids entering the tank. This is accomplished very easily with *level control*.

In a level control scheme, a level indicator provides a signal proportional to the height of the liquid level in the tank. This signal is compared with the set-point signal (desired liquid level), and the difference signal is fed back to electronic control valves that control the input liquid flow rates to the tank.

There are several methods of indicating liquid level in a tank. We will examine two of the simplest methods. They are the *variable resistance* method and the *linear voltage differential transformer* (LVDT) method.

The variable resistance method is demonstrated in Fig. 9-28. A vertical rod is attached at one end to a float. The other end of the rod is attached to the wiper of a variable resistor or potentiometer. A potential is applied across the resistor. As the liquid level changes, the position of the wiper changes as does the voltage at the wiper. Thus, liquid level is transformed into a voltage reading. More accurate variations of this method include the use of the variable resistance in one arm of a Wheatstone bridge, as shown in Fig. 9-29.

The principal drawback to this method is mechanical wear of the variable resistance. After a relatively short operating time, the variable resistor must be

131

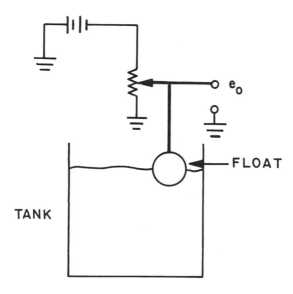

Fig. 9-28. The variable resistance method of indicating liquid level.

changed since the abrasive action of the wiper tends to destroy the resistor.

A much better method of determining liquid level (or any linear displacement) involves use of the linear

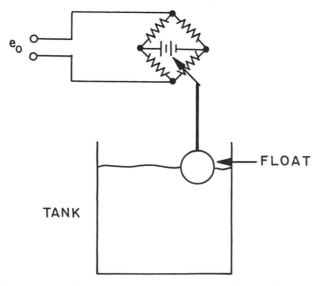

Fig. 9-29. The variable resistance method of indicating liquid level, employing a Wheatstone bridge.

voltage differential transformer, or LVDT. In fact, the LVDT is the transducer of choice in almost all applications where position or linear displacement must be measured. This method is shown in Fig. 9-30.

A central coil excited by an ac signal is connected to the vertical float rod. As the level changes, the coil's position between the pair of coils is altered. If the moving coil is centered between the pair, equal voltages are induced in both. The rectified signals from the pair are of equal magnitudes, so that the output signal is zero. If, however, the moving coil is not centered between the pair, voltages of unequal magnitudes are induced in the pair of coils, and the output signal is nonzero (either positive or negative). This signal, then, is used to indicate liquid level, and is fed to the process control equipment.

The output from an LVDT is not linear over all ranges, as is shown in Fig. 9-31. However, with a little care in designing the LVDT, the output can be made linear over a reasonably broad range.

The completed level control scheme, employing proportional-integral control, is shown in Fig. 9-32. In

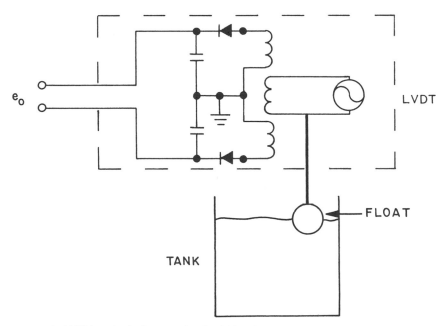

Fig. 9-30. LVDT method of measuring liquid level.

133

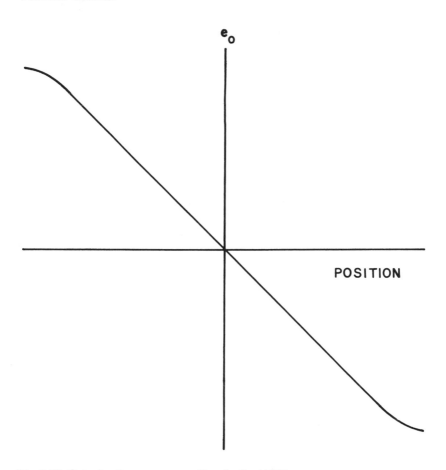

Fig. 9-31. Output voltage versus position for the LVDT.

this example it is assumed that process demands control the outflow from the tank. In other words, our only degree of freedom in controlling tank level is derived from control of flow rate of liquid entering the tank. The LVDT (or variable resistance) provides a signal that is proportional to liquid level, which is compared with the set-point signal (from the voltage reference source). This output is integrated and added to itself, thus providing a proportional-integral control signal to the electronic control valve. Because of the tank's capacity, oscillations are not a problem, so that derivative action is unnecessary.

Fuel-Air Metering Control For Furnaces

Almost all combustion devices, from the internal

combustion engine of an automobile to the combustion furnace of an industrial power boiler, require an appropriate fuel-to-air ratio for maximum efficiency. In this example, we consider a process control loop for fuel to air ratio. This loop is not the only control loop for the furnace, since the amount of fuel required will be controlled by the demands of the process. That is, the process demand will be the set point for fuel flow, and the set point will vary as process demands change.

Figure 9-33 shows a furnace whose fuel flow rate is controlled by a proportional-integral controller. It is assumed that this is a furnace generating steam for the production of electrical power. As demand for electrical power increases (i.e., as the set point changes), the proportional-integral controller increases fuel flow to the furnace.

In this particular system, only the fuel flow to the furnace changes as demand changes. The air flow remains constant, so that the fuel-to-air ratio departs from the optimum value. The result is a mixture that is either fuel-rich, with incomplete combustion, wasted fuel and increased pollution, or fuel-lean, with insufficient power generation.

This situation can be remedied with the control

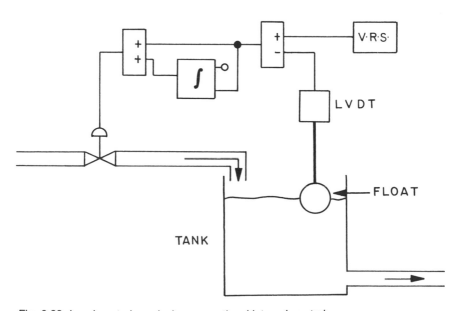

Fig. 9-32. Level control employing proportional-integral control.

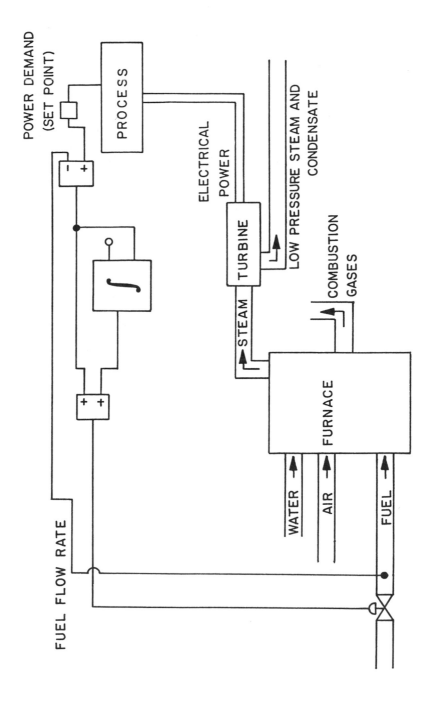

Fig. 9-33. Power boiler proportional-integral control for fuel flow.

scheme shown in Fig. 9-34. Both fuel and air flow rates are measured (see Chapter 8 for flow-rate measurement techniques) and the ratio is obtained with a divider (Chapter 5). This ratio is compared with the set-point value, which is provided by a voltage reference source. This error signal is integrated and added to itself, and used to feed an electronic control valve in the air flow line.

This example indicates some of the complexities of process control in industry. Many control loops are used to control one piece of equipment, and the effect of controlling one variable (such as fuel flow) on another (such as fuel-to-air ratio) must be considered.

Steam Pressure Control

Steam pressure control is often critical not only for process efficiency but also for safety. If the pressure limit of a vessel is exceeded, it can explode. For this reason, oscillations in steam pressure are not desired, and proportional-integral-derivative control is indicated.

A simple control scheme is shown in Fig. 9-35. In this figure, all the considerations of fuel flow, fuel-to-air ratio and ignition signal are represented schematically by the firing rate controller block. This has been done to simplify the figure.

A pressure transducer in the steam line indicates the steam pressure, and the signal from this transducer is compared with the set-point value. The error signal is then subjected to integration and differentiation, and the combined signal is then fed to the firing rate controller.

An added complication occurs when process demand is considered. This is illustrated in Fig. 9-36. When the demand for steam changes rapidly, steam pressure tends to fluctuate. In the system shown in the figure, total steam demand will control the fuel flow rate. (Fuel-to-air ratio is controlled in the firing rate controller block.) The steam pressure feedback loop acts as a trimming control. The multiplier is an appropriate control element since the amount of correction necessary for a given deviation in steam pressure is proportional to process steam demand (or load). By multiplying the signals, we are using one control signal to compensate equally for both process demand and pressure variations.

Most plants use more than one steam or power

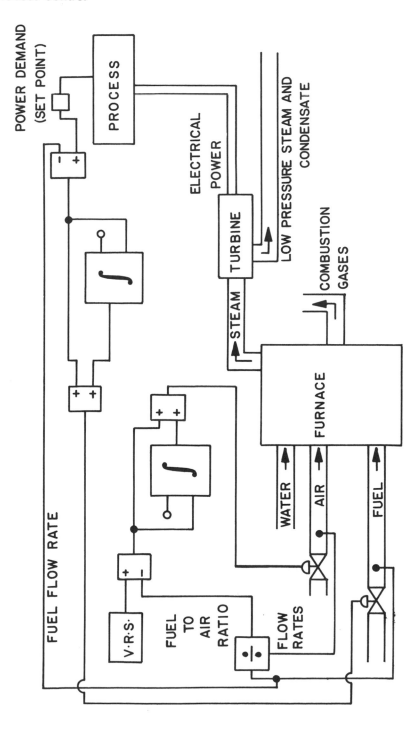

Fig. 9-34. Power boiler with proportional-integral control for fuel flow and proportional-integral control for fuel-to-air ratio control.

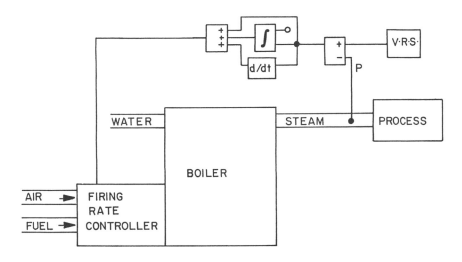

Fig. 9-35. Proportional-integral-derivative control of steam pressure.

boiler. This rapidly complicates the control scheme. The general principles outlined above, however, are still utilized in controlling steam pressure and flow.

Effluent Discharge Control

Many process industries use large quantities of water. That is why so many industries are located near lakes or rivers. After the water used in manufacturing is recovered, it is cleaned up and discharged back into the river or lake. Strict regulations are in effect regarding the discharge of process water. The biological oxygen demand (BOD) of the discharged water is limited to certain ranges, the color of the discharged water is monitored, and the effects of discharged water pH and temperature on river (or lake) pH and temperature are strictly controlled.

In this example it will be assumed that all of the above effects may be controlled by adjusting the water discharge rate to some optimum value compared with river flow rate. In other words, it will be assumed that there exists a ratio of discharged water volume to river water volume which is an optimum for control of BOD, color, pH and temperature. The essence of the control scheme will then be control of effluent volumetric flow rate. The feedback signal will be proportional to the river volumetric flow rate.

139

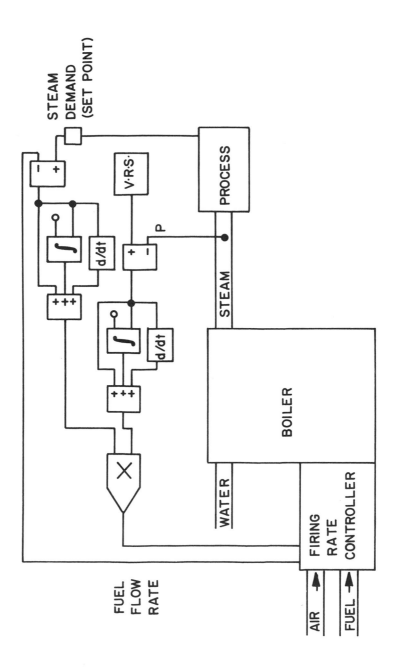

Fig. 9-36. Proportional-integral-derivative control of steam pressure and steam demand.

Three things are needed to determine the volumetric flow rate of the river. They are: river velocity, river level, and river width. This is shown schematically in Fig. 9-37.

If it is assumed that the river has a smooth, level bottom of known width, then the height of the river (river level) multiplied by the width will give the cross sectional river area (shaded portion in Fig. 9-37). Multiplication of this area by river velocity gives the volume of water flowing past the shaded area for a given time. For example, assuming river level is three feet, river width is ten feet, and river velocity is 60 feet per minute, the volumetric flow rate is

$$Q = 3 \text{ ft} \times 10 \text{ ft} \times 60 \text{ ft/min}$$
$$= 1800 \text{ cubic feet per minute} \qquad \textbf{(9-8)}$$

Using the conversion factor of 7.48 liquid gallons per cubic foot yields

$$Q = 1800 \times 7.48 = 13{,}464 \text{ gallons per minute} \qquad \textbf{(9-9)}$$

In general, river level and river velocity are not completely independent. That is, a higher river velocity will most likely be found when river level is higher than normal. In order to assure proper calculation of volumetric flow rate, both river level and river velocity should be measured.

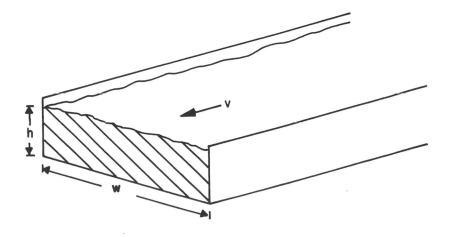

Fig. 9-37. Calculation of river volumetric flow rate.

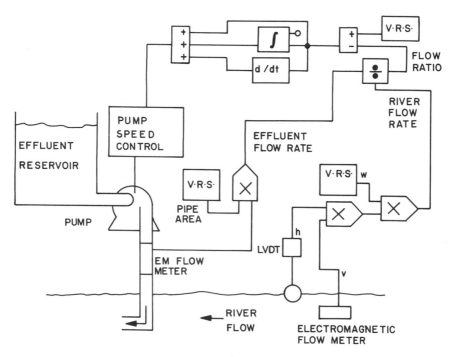

Fig. 9-38. Effluent discharge control scheme.

In the effluent control system to be presented, a pump will be used to move the effluent from the reservoir to the river. The gallonage moved by the pump can be controlled continuously from zero gallons per minute to the pump maximum value by the pump speed control unit.

The control scheme is shown in Fig. 9-38. Electromagnetic type flow meters are used to measure river velocity and effluent velocity. Effluent velocity is multiplied by pipe cross-sectional area (previously measured, with signal provided by a voltage reference source) to obtain effluent volumetric flow rate. This signal becomes the numerator fed to a divider module.

The river velocity signal (from the electromagnetic flow meter) is multiplied by river level, and this product is multiplied by river width (previously measured, with signal provided by a voltage reference source). This signal, the river volumetric flow rate, is fed to the divider module, where it becomes the denominator. The output of the divider module is the ratio of effluent volumetric flow rate to river volumetric flow rate.

142

The ratio of effluent volumetric flow rate to river volumetric flow rate is now compared with the optimum value (from a voltage reference source). The error signal is subjected to proportional-integral-derivative treatment, and the control signal is fed to the speed control box for the pump. Deviations from the ideal ratio are corrected by adjusting effluent flow rate.

CONCLUDING THOUGHTS

This chapter has provided only a hint as to how the analog computational circuits described in this book can be used. Any thorough treatment of process control will necessarily involve the use of Laplace transforms. An introduction to Laplace transforms was considered beyond the scope of this book. Further information on the subject can be found in the texts listed in the Bibliography.

Appendix

Integrated Circuit Data Sheets

This Appendix contains information on the AD533, 755, and the 759N and 759P, courtesy of Analog Devices; the 4423, courtesy of Burr-Brown; and the LF353, courtesy of National Semiconductor.

Low Cost IC
Multiplier,Divider,Squarer,Square Rooter

AD533

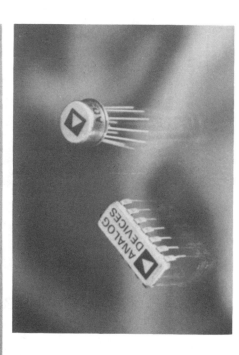

ANALOG DEVICES

FEATURES
Simplicity of Operation: Only
    Four External Adjustments
Max 4-Quadrant Error Below 0.5%
    (AD533L)
Low Temperature Drift: 0.01%/°C
    (AD533L)
Multiplies, Divides, Squares, Square Roots

PRODUCT DESCRIPTION
The Analog Devices AD533 is a low cost integrated circuit multiplier comprised of a transconductance multiplying element, stable reference, and output amplifier on a monolithic silicon chip. Specified accuracy is easily achieved by the straight-forward adjustment of feedthrough, output zero, and gain trim pots. The AD533 multiplies in four quadrants with a transfer function of XY/10V, divides in two quadrants with a 10VZ/X transfer function, and square roots in one

The low cost and simplicity of operation of the AD533 make it especially well suited for use in such widespread applications as modulation and demodulation, automatic gain control and phase detection. Other applications include frequency discrimination, rms computation, peak detection, voltage controlled oscillators and filters, function generation, and power measurements.

All models are available in the hermetically sealed TO-100 metal can and TO-116 ceramic DIP packages.

146

quadrant with a transfer function of $-\sqrt{10VZ}$. Several levels of accuracy are provided: the AD533J, AD533K, and AD533L, for 0 to +70°C operation, are specified for maximum multiplying errors of 2%, 1%, and 0.5% respectively at +25°C. The AD533S, for operation from –55°C to +125°C, is guaranteed for a maximum 1% multiplying error at +25°C. The maximum error specification is a true measure of overall accuracy since it includes the effects of offset voltage, feedthrough, scale factor, and nonlinearity in all four quadrants.

The low drift design of the AD533 insures that high accuracy is maintained with variations in temperature. The op amp output provides ±10 volts at 5mA, and is fully protected against short circuits to ground or either supply voltage: all inputs are fully protected against over-voltage transients with internal series resistors. The devices provide excellent ac performance, with typical small signal bandwidth of 1.0MHz, full power bandwidth of 750kHz, and slew rate of 45V/μs.

P.O. Box 280; Norwood, Massachusetts 02062 U.S.A.
Tel: 617/329-4700   Twx: 710/394-6577
Telex: 924491   Cables: ANALOG NORWOODMASS

SPECIFICATIONS (typical @ +25°C, externally trimmed and $V_S = \pm15V$ dc unless otherwise specified)

PARAMETER	CONDITIONS	AD533J	AD533K	AD533L	AD533S
ABSOLUTE MAX RATINGS					
Internal Power Dissipation		500mW	*	*	*
Input Voltage[1]					
$X_{in}, Y_{in}, Z_{in}, X_o, Y_o, Z_o$		$\pm V_S$	*	*	*
Rated Operating Temp Range		0 to +70°C	*	*	-55°C to +125°C
Storage Temp Range		-65°C to +150°C	*	*	*
Output Short Circuit	To Ground	Indefinite	*	*	*
MULTIPLIER SPECIFICATIONS					
Transfer Function		$XY/10V$	*	*	*
	Untrimmed	$XY/6V$ max $[XY/10V$ min]	*	*	*
Total Error (of full scale)	T_A = min to max	±2.0% max	±1.0% max	±0.5% max	±1.0% max
vs. Temperature	T_A = min to max	±3.0%	±2.0%	±1.0%	±1.5%
		±0.04%/°C	±0.03%/°C	±0.01%/°C	±0.01%/°C
Nonlinearity					
X Input	$V_x = V_o = 20V(p\text{-}p)$	±0.8%	±0.5%	**	**
Y Input	$V_y = V_o = 20V(p\text{-}p)$	±0.3%	±0.2%	**	**
Feedthrough					
X Input	$V_x = 20V(p\text{-}p)$, $V_y = 0$, f = 50Hz	200mV (p-p) max	150mV(p-p) max	50mV(p-p) max	100mV (p-p) max
Y Input	$V_y = 20V(p\text{-}p)$, $V_x = 0$, f = 50Hz	200mV(p-p) max	150mV(p-p) max	50mV(p-p) max	100mV (p-p) max
DIVIDER SPECIFICATIONS					
Transfer Function		$10VZ/X$	*	*	*
	Untrimmed	$10VZ/X$ max $[6VZ/X$ min]			
Total Error (of full scale)	$V_x = -10V$ dc, $V_z = \pm10V$ dc	±1.0%	±0.5%	±0.2%	±0.5%
	$V_x = -1V$ dc, $V_z = \pm10V$ dc	±3.0%	±2.0%	±1.5%	±2.0%
SQUARER SPECIFICATIONS					
Transfer Function		$X^2/10V$	*	*	*
	Untrimmed	$X^2/6V$ max $[X^2/10V$ min]			
Total Error (of full scale)		±0.8%	±0.4%	±0.2%	±0.4%
SQUARE ROOTER SPECIFICATIONS					
Transfer Function		$-\sqrt{10VZ}$	*	*	*
	Untrimmed	$-\sqrt{10VZ}$ max $[-\sqrt{6VZ}$ min]			
Total Error (of full scale)		±0.8%	±0.4%	±0.2%	±0.4%
INPUT SPECIFICATIONS					
Input Resistance					
X Input		10MΩ	*	*	*
Y Input		6MΩ	*	*	*

Parameter	Conditions				
Z Input		36kΩ	*	*	*
Input Bias Current					
X, Y Inputs		3µA	7.5µA max	5µA max	7.5µA max
Z Input		±25µA	10µA	7µA	7µA
X, Y Inputs	T_A = min to max	12µA	*	*	*
Z Input	T_A = min to max	±35µA	*	*	*
Input Voltage V_X, V_Y, V_Z	For Rated Accuracy	±10V	*	*	*
DYNAMIC SPECIFICATIONS					
Small Signal, Unity Gain		1.0MHz	*	*	*
Full Power Bandwidth		750kHz	*	*	*
Slew Rate		45V/µs	*	*	*
Small Signal Amplitude Error	0.5° phase shift	1% at 75kHz	*	*	*
Sm Sig 1% Vector Error		5kHz	*	*	*
Settling Time	±10V step	1µs to 2%	*	*	*
Overload Recovery		2µs to 2%	*	*	*
OUTPUT AMPLIFIER SPECIFICATIONS					
Output Impedance		100Ω	*	*	*
Output Voltage Swing	T_A = min to max, $R_L \geq 2k\Omega$, $C_L \leq 1000pF$	±10V min	*	*	*
Output Noise	f = 5Hz to 10kHz	0.6mV(rms)	*	*	*
	f = 5Hz to 5MHz	3.0mV(rms)	*	*	*
Output Offset Voltage		Trimmable To Zero	*	*	*
vs. Temperature	T_A = min to max	0.7mV/°C	*	*	*
POWER SUPPLY SPECIFICATIONS					
Supply Voltage	Rated Performance	±15V	*	*	*
	Operating	±15V to ±18V	±10V to ±18V	±10V to ±18V	±10V to ±22V
Supply Current	Quiescent	±6mA max	*	*	*
Power Supply Variation	*Includes* Effects of Recommended Null Pots				
Multiplier Accuracy		±0.5%/%	*	*	*
Output Offset		±10mV/%	*	*	*
Scale Factor		±0.1%/%	*	*	*
Feedthrough		±10mV/%	*	*	*

NOTES

[1] Max input voltage is zero when supplies are turned off.

*Specifications same as AD533J.

**Specifications same as AD533K.

Specifications subject to change without notice.

Applying the AD533

MULTIPLIER

Multiplier operation is accomplished by closing the loop around the internal op amp with the Z input connected to the output. The X_O null pot balances the X input channel to minimize Y feedthrough and similarly the Y_O pot minimizes the X feedthrough. The Z_O pot nulls the output op amp offset voltage and the gain pot sets the full scale output level.

DIVIDER

The divide mode utilizes the multiplier in a fed-back configuration where the Y input now controls the feedback factor. With X = full scale, the gain (V_O/Z) becomes unity after trimming. Reducing the X input reduces the feedback around the op amp by a like amount, thereby increasing the gain. This reciprocal relationship forms the basis of the divide mode. Accuracy and bandwidth decrease as the denominator decreases.

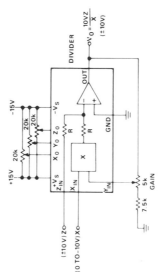

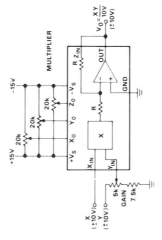

TRIM PROCEDURES

1. With X = Y = 0 volts, adjust Z_O for 0V dc output.
2. With Y = 20 volts p-p (at f = 50Hz) and X = 0V, adjust X_O for minimum ac output.
3. With X = 20 volts p-p (at f = 50Hz) and Y = 0V, adjust Y_O for minimum ac output.
4. Readjust Z_O for 0V dc output.
5. With X = +10V dc and Y = 20 volts p-p (at f = 50Hz), adjust gain for output = Y_{in}.

NOTE: For best accuracy over limited voltage ranges (e.g., ±5V), gain and feedthrough adjustments should be optimized with the inputs in the desired range, as linearity is considerably better over smaller ranges of input.

TRIM PROCEDURES

1. Set all pots at mid-scale.
2. With Z = 0V, trim Z_O to hold the output constant, as X is varied from –10V dc through –1V dc.
3. With Z = 0V, X = –10V dc, trim Y_O for 0V dc.
4. With Z = X or –X, trim X_O for the minimum worst-case variations as X is varied from –10V dc to –1V dc.
5. Repeat steps 2 and 3 if step 4 required a large initial adjustment.
6. With Z = X or –X, trim the gain for the closest average approach to ±10V dc output as X is varied from –10V dc to –3V dc.

SQUARER

Squarer operation is a special case of multiplier operation where the X and Y inputs are connected together and two quadrant operation results since the output is always positive. When the X and Y inputs are connected together, a composite offset results which is the algebraic sum of the individual offsets which can be nulled using the X_O pot alone.

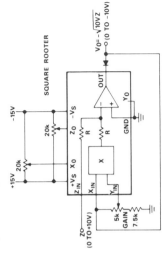

TRIM PROCEDURES

1. With X = 0 volts, adjust Z_O for 0V dc output.
2. With X = +10V dc, adjust gain for +10V dc output.
3. Reverse polarity of X input and adjust X_O to reduce the output error to ½ its original value, readjust the gain to take out the remaining error.
4. Check the output offset with input grounded. If nonzero, repeat the above procedure until no errors remain.

SQUARE ROOTER

This mode is also a fed-back configuration with both the X and Y inputs tied to the op amp output through an external diode to prevent latchup. Accuracy, noise and frequency response are proportional to $\sqrt{Z}$, which implies a wider usable dynamic range than the divide mode.

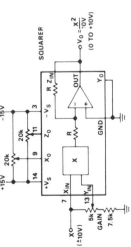

TRIM PROCEDURES

1. With Z = +0.1V dc, adjust Z_O for Output = −1.0V dc.
2. With Z = +10.0V dc, adjust gain for Output = −10.0V dc.
3. With Z = +2.0V dc, adjust X_O for Output = −4.47 ±0.1V dc.
4. Repeat steps 2 and 3, if necessary. Repeat step 1.

151

TYPICAL PERFORMANCE CHARACTERISTICS

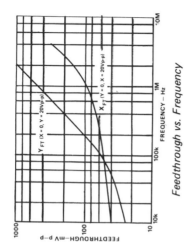

Feedthrough vs. Frequency

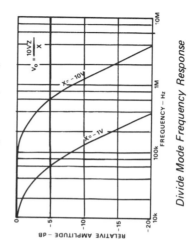

Divide Mode Frequency Response

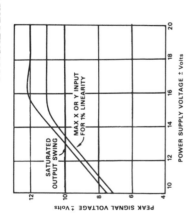

Allowable Signal Swing vs. Supply Voltage

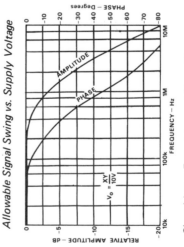

Closed Loop Frequency and Phase Response

PIN CONFIGURATION & DIMENSIONS
Dimensions shown in inches and (mm).

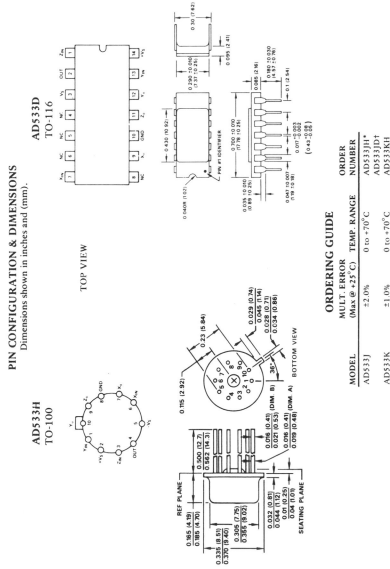

AD533H
TO-100

TOP VIEW

AD533D
TO-116

ORDERING GUIDE

MODEL	MULT. ERROR (Max @ +25°C)	TEMP. RANGE	ORDER NUMBER
AD533J	±2.0%	0 to +70°C	AD533JH* AD533JD†
AD533K	±1.0%	0 to +70°C	AD533KH AD533KD
AD533L	±0.5%	0 to +70°C	AD533LH AD533LD
AD533S	±1.0%	−55°C to +125°C	AD533SH AD533SD

*TO-100 metal can package
†TO-116 ceramic DIP package

ANALOG DEVICES

6-Decade, High Accuracy Log, Antilog Amplifiers

MODELS 755N, 755P

FEATURES
Complete Log/Antilog Amplifier.
External Components Not Required;
Internal Reference; Temperature Compensated
6 Decades Current Operation — 1nA to 1mA
1/2% max Error — 10nA to 100μA
1% max Error — 1nA to 1mA
4 Decades Voltage Operation — 1mV to 10V
1/2% max Error — 1mV to 1V
1% max Error — 1mV to 10V

APPLICATIONS
Log Current or Voltage
Antilog Voltage
Data Compression or Expansion
Absorbence Measurements
Computing Powers and Log Ratios

GENERAL DESCRIPTION
Model 755 is a complete dc logarithmic amplifier consisting of an accurate temperature compensated antilog element, and a low bias current FET amplifier. In addition to offering 120dB of current logging (1nA to 1mA) and 80dB of voltage logging (1mV to 10V), the 755 features exceptionally low bias currents of 10pA and 15μV/°C voltage drift to satisfy most wide range voltage is also presented to illustrate the log amplifier's transfer characteristics.

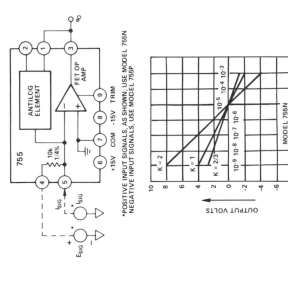

Figure 1. Functional Block Diagram and Transfer Function

applications. Conformance to ideal log operation is held to ±1% over its total 120dB current range (1nA to 1mA), with ±0.5% conformity guaranteed over an 80dB range (10nA to 100μA). Two models are available, model 755N and model 755P. The N version computes the log of positive input signals and the P version computes the log of negative input signals.

Advanced design techniques and improved component selection are used to obtain exceptionally good performance. For example, the use of monolithic devices greatly reduces the influence of temperature variations. Offering both log and antilog operation, model 755's price and performance are especially attractive as an alternative to in-house designs of OEM applications. This log design also improves significantly over competitive designs in price, performance, and package size.

MAJOR IMPROVEMENTS IN I_{os}

For most low level applications, the input bias current I_{os}, is especially critical, since it is the major source of error when processing low level currents. At 1nA of input current there is an error contribution of 1% for every 10pA of I_{os}. Recognizing the importance of this parameter, bias current of model 755 is maintained below 10pA.

APPLICATIONS

When connected in the current or voltage logging configuration, as shown in Figure 1, the model 755 may be used in several key applications. A plot of input current versus output

Information furnished by Analog Devices is believed to be accurate and reliable. However, no responsibility is assumed by Analog Devices for its use; nor for any infringements of patents or other rights of third parties which may result from its use. No license is granted by implication or otherwise under any patent or patent rights of Analog Devices.

P.O. Box 280; Norwood, Massachusetts 02062 U.S.A.
Telex: 924491   Cables: ANALOG NORWOODMASS

SPECIFICATIONS (typical @ +25°C and ±15V dc unless otherwise noted)

MODEL	755N/P
TRANSFER FUNCTIONS	
Current Mode	$e_O = -Klog_{10}\dfrac{I_{SIG}}{I_{REF}}$
Voltage Mode	$e_O = -Klog_{10}\dfrac{E_{SIG}}{E_{REF}}$
Antilog Mode	$e_O = E_{REF}\, 10^{-\left(\frac{E_{SIG}}{K}\right)}$

TRANSFER FUNCTION PARAMETERS

Scale Factor (K) Selections[1,2]	2, 1, 2/3 Volt/Decade
Error @ +25°C	±1% max
vs. Temperature (0 to +70°C)	±0.04%/°C max
Reference Voltage (E_{REF})[2]	0.1V
Error @ +25°C	±3% max
vs. Temperature (0 to +70°C)	±0.1%/°C max
Reference Current (I_{REF})[2]	10µA
Error @ +25°C	±3% max
vs. Temperature (0 to +70°C)	±0.1%/°C max

LOG CONFORMITY ERROR

I_{SIG} Range	E_{SIG} Range	R.T.I.	R.T.O. (K = 1)
1nA to 10nA	—	±1% max	±4.3mV max
10nA to 100µA	1mV to 1V	±0.5% max	±2.17mV max
100µA to 1mA	1V to 10V	±1% max	±4.3mV max
1nA to 1mA	—	±1% max	±4.3mV max

INPUT SPECIFICATIONS

Current Signal Range	
Model 755N	+1nA to +1mA min
Model 755P	-1nA to -1mA min
Max Safe Input Current	±10mA max
Bias Current @ +25°C	(0, +) 10pA max
vs. Temperature (0 to +70°C)	x2/+10°C
Voltage Signal Range (Log Mode)	
Model 755N	+1mV to +10V min
Model 755P	-1mV to -10V min
Voltage Signal Range, Antilog Mode	
Model 755N, 755P	$-2 \leqslant \dfrac{E_{SIG}}{K} \leqslant 2$
Offset Voltage @ +25°C (Adjustable to 0)	±400µV max
vs. Temperature (0 to +70°C)	±15µV/°C max
vs. Supply Voltage	±15µV/%

OUTLINE DIMENSIONS

Dimensions shown in inches and (mm).

1.51 MAX (38.1) — 0.41 MAX (10.4) — 0.2 TO 0.25 MAX (5 TO 6.4) — 1.51 MAX (38.1) — 0.04 DIA (1.02) — 0.1 GRID (2.5)

755

BOTTOM VIEW

9 TRIM — 8 -15 — 7 COM — 6 +15 — 5 I_{SIG} — 4 E_{SIG} — 3 e_{OUT} — 2 2V/DEC — 1 1V/DEC

P* — 100k

*Optional 100kΩ external trim pot — ADI PN79PR100k. Input offset voltage may be adjusted to zero with trim pot connected as shown. With trim terminal 9 left open, input offset voltage will be ±0.4mV maximum.

MATING SOCKET AC1016

TRANSFER CURVES

Plot of Output Voltage vs Input Voltage for Model 755 Connected in the Log Mode

Plot of Output Voltage vs Input Current for Model 755 Connected in the Log Mode

FREQUENCY RESPONSE, Sinewave
Small Signal Bandwidth, –3dB

I_{SIG} = 1nA	80Hz
I_{SIG} = 1μA	10kHz
I_{SIG} = 10μA	40kHz
I_{SIG} = 1mA	100kHz

RISE TIME
Increasing Input Current

10nA to 100nA	100μs
100nA to 1μA	7μs
1μA to 1mA	4μs

Decreasing Input Current

1mA to 1μA	7μs
1μA to 100nA	30μs
100nA to 10nA	400μs

INPUT NOISE

Voltage, 10Hz to 10kHz	2μV rms
Current, 10Hz to 10kHz	2pA rms

OUTPUT SPECIFICATIONS[3]
Rated Output

Voltage	±10V min
Current	
Log Mode	±5mA
Antilog Mode	±4mA
Resistance	0.5Ω

POWER SUPPLY[4]

Rated Performance	±15V dc
Operating	±(12 to 18)V dc
Current, Quiescent	±7mA

TEMPERATURE RANGE

Rated Performance	0 to +70°C
Operating	–25°C to +85°C
Storage	–55°C to +125°C

CASE SIZE	1.5″ x 1.5″ x 0.4″

[1] Use terminal 1 for K = 1V/decade; terminal 2 for K = 2V/decade; terminals 1 or 2 (shorted together) for K = 2/3V/decade.
[2] Specification is + for model 755N; – for model 755P.
[3] No damage due to any pin being shorted to ground.
[4] Recommended power supply, model 904, ±15V @ ±50mA output.
Specifications subject to change without notice.

157

PRINCIPLE OF OPERATION

Log operation is obtained by placing the antilog element in the feedback loop of the op amp as shown in Figure 1. At the summing junction, terminal 5, the input signal current to be processed is summed with the output current of the antilog element. To attain a balance of these two currents, the op amp provides the required output voltage to the antilog feedback element. Under these conditions the ideal transfer equation (K = 1) is:

$$e_{OUT} = 1V \log_{10} I_{SIG}/I_{REF}$$

The log is a mathematical operator which is defined only for numbers, which are dimensionless quantities. Since an input current would have the dimensions of amperes it must be referenced to another current, I_{REF}, the ratio being dimensionless. For this purpose a temperature compensated reference of $10\mu A$ is generated internally.

The scale factor, K, is a multiplying constant. For a change in input current of one decade (decade = ratio of 10:1), the output changes by K volts. K may be selected as 1V or 2V by connecting the output to pin 1 or 2, respectively. If the output is connected to both pins 1 and 2, K will be 2/3V.

A graph of the ideal transfer function for model 755N is presented in Figure 2, for one decade of operation. Although specific values of i_{in} and e_{out} are presented for n = 1, other values may be plotted by varying n.

The change in output, due to a 1% input change is a constant value of ±4.3mV. Conversely, a dc error at the output of ±4.3mV is equivalent to a change at the input of 1%. An abbreviated table is presented below for converting between errors referred to output (R.T.O.), and errors referred to input (R.T.I.).

TABLE 1

Error. R.T.I. (N)	Error R.T.O.		
	K = 1	K = 2	K = 2/3
0.1%	0.43mV	0.86mV	0.28mV
0.5	2.17	4.34	1.45
1.0	4.32	8.64	2.88
3.0	12.84	25.68	8.56
4.0	17.03	34.06	11.35
5.0	21.19	42.38	14.13
10.0	41.39	82.78	27.59

Table 1. Converting Output Error in mV to Input Error in %
NOTE:
Data may be interpolated with reasonable accuracy, for small errors by adding various values of N and their corresponding R.T.O. terms. That is, for N = 2.5% and K = 1, combine 2% and 0.5% terms to obtain 10.77mV.

SOURCES OF ERROR

When applying the model 755, a firm understanding of error sources associated with log amplifiers is beneficial for achieving maximum performance. The definitions, limiations and compensation techniques for errors specified on log amplifiers will be discussed here.

Log Conformity Error – Log conformity in logarithmic devices is a specification similar to linearity in linear devices. Log conformity error is the difference between the value of the transfer equation and the actual value which occurs at the output of the log module, after scale factor, reference and offset errors are eliminated or taken into account. For model 755, the best linearity performance is obtained in the middle 4 decades (10nA to 100μA). For this range, log conformity error is ±0.5% R.T.I. or 2.17mV R.T.O. To obtain optimum performance, the input data should be scaled to this range.

Offset Voltage (E_{os}) – The offset voltage, E_{os}, of model 755 is the offset voltage of the internal FET amplifier. This voltage appears as a small dc offset voltage in series with the input terminals. For current logging applications, its error contribution is negligible. However, for log voltage applications, best performance is obtained by an offset trim adjustment.

Offset Current (I_{os}) – The offset current, I_{os}, of model 755 is the bias current of the internal FET amplifier. This parameter can be a significant source of error when processing signals in the nanoamp region. For this reason, I_{os}, for model 755, is held within a conservative 10pA max.

Reference Current (I_{REF}) – I_{REF} is the internally generated current source to which all input currents are compared. I_{REF} tolerance errors appear as a dc offset at the output. The specified value of I_{REF} is ±3%, referred to the input, and, from Table 1, corresponds to a dc offset of ±12.84mV, for K = 1. This offset is independent of input signal and may be removed by injecting a current into terminal 1 or 2.

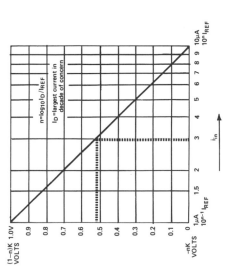

Figure 2. Input vs. Output for Any One Decade of Operation

REFERRING ERRORS TO INPUT

A unique property of log amplifiers is that a dc error of any given amount at the output corresponds to a constant percent of the input, regardless of input level. To illustrate this, consider the output effects due to changing the input by 1%.

The output would be:

$$e_{out} = 1V \log_{10} (I_{SIG}/I_{REF})(1.01) \text{ which is equivalent to:}$$

$$e_{out} = \underbrace{1V \log_{10} I_{SIG}/I_{REF}}_{\text{Initial Value}} \underbrace{\pm 1V \log_{10} 1.01}_{\text{Change}}$$

159

ANTILOG OPERATION

The model 755 may be used to develop the antilog of the input voltage when connected as shown in Figure 4. The antilog transfer function (an exponential), is:

$$e_{out} = E_{REF}\ 10^{-e_{in}/K}$$

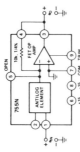

Figure 4. Functional Block Diagram

Principle of Operation – The antilog element converts the voltage input, appearing at terminal 1 or 2, to a current which is proportional to the antilog of the applied voltage. The current-to-voltage conversion is then completed by the feedback resistor in a closed-loop op amp circuit.

A more complete expression for the antilog function is:

$$e_{out} = E_{REF}\ 10^{-e_{in}/K} + E_{OS}$$

The terms K, E_{OS}, and E_{REF} are those described previously in the LOG section.

Offset Voltage (E_{os}) Adjustment – Although offset voltage of the antilog circuit may be balanced by connecting it in the log mode, and using the technique described previously, it may be more advantageous to use the circuit of Figure 5. In this configuration, offset voltage is equal to $e_{out}/100$. Adjust for the desired null, using the 100k trim pot. After adjusting, turn power off, remove the external 100Ω resistor, and the jumper from pin 1 to +15V. For 755P, use the same procedure but connect pin 1 to –15V.

Reference Voltage (E_{REF}) – E_{REF} is the effective internally generated voltage to which all input voltages are compared. It is related to I_{REF} through the equation:

$$E_{REF} = I_{REF} \times R_{in}$$

where R_{in} is an internal $10k\Omega$, precision resistor. Virtually all tolerance in E_{REF} is due to I_{REF}. Consequently, variations in I_{REF} cause a shift in E_{REF}.

Scale Factor (K) – Scale factor is the voltage change at the output for a decade (i.e., 10:1) change at the input, when connected in the log mode. Error in scale factor is equivalent to a change in gain, or slope, and is specified in per cent of the nominal value. An external adjustment may be performed if fine trimming is desired for improved accuracy.

EXTERNAL ADJUSTMENTS FOR LOG OPERATION (OPTIONAL)

Trimming E_{os} – The amplifier's offset voltage, E_{os}, may be trimmed for improved accuracy with the model 755 connected in its log circuit. To accomplish this, a $100k\Omega$, 10 turn pot is connected as shown in Figure 3, and the input terminal, pin 4, is connected to ground. Under these conditions the output voltage is:

$$e_{out} = -K\ log_{10}\ E_{os}/E_{REF}$$

To obtain an offset voltage of $100\mu V$ or less, for K = 1, the trim pot should be adjusted until the output voltage is between +3 and +4 volts for model 755N, and –3 to –4V for model 755P.

For other values of K, the trim pot should be adjusted for an output of $e_{out} = 3 \times K$ to $4 \times K$ where K is the scale factor.

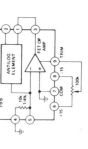

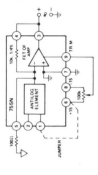

Figure 3. Trimming E_{OS} in Log Mode

REFERENCE CURRENT OR REFERENCE VOLTAGE

The reference current or voltage of model 755 may be shifted by injecting a constant current into the unused scale factor terminal (pin 1 or pin 2). Each 66μA of current injected will shift the reference one decade, in accordance with the expression: $I_I = 66\mu A \log 10\mu A/I_{REF}$, where I_I = current to be injected and I_{REF} = the desired reference current.

By changing I_{REF}, there is a corresponding change in E_{REF} since, $E_{REF} = I_{REF} \times R_{in}$. An alternate method for rescaling E_{REF} is to connect an external R_{in}, at the I_{in} terminal (pin 5) to supplant the 10kΩ supplied internally (leaving it unconnected). The expression for E_{REF} is then, $E_{REF} = R_{in}I_{REF}$. Care must be taken to choose R_{in} such that $(e_{in} \max)/R_{in}$ ⩽1mA.

Scale Factor (K) Adjustment – Scale factor may be increased from its nominal value by inserting a series resistor between the output terminal, pin 3, and either terminal 1 or 2. The table below should be consulted when making these scale factor changes.

TABLE 2

Range of K	Connect Series R to Pin	Value of R	Note
2/3V to 1.01V	1	15kΩ x (K – 2/3)	use pins 1, 2
1.01V to 2.02V	1	15kΩ x (K – 1)	use pin 1
> 2.02V	2	15kΩ x (K – 2)	use pin 2

Table 2. Resistor Selection Chart for Shifting Scale Factor

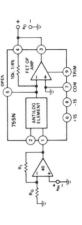

Figure 5. Trimming E_{OS} in Antilog Mode

Reference Voltage (E_{REF}) Adjustment – In antilog operation, the voltage reference appears as a multiplying constant. E_{REF} adjustment may be accomplished by connecting a resistor, R, from pin 5 to pin 3, in place of the internal 10kΩ. The value of R is determined by:

$$R = E_{REF} \text{ desired}/10^{-5} \text{ A}$$

Scale Factor (K) Adjustment – The scale factor may be adjusted for all values of K greater than 2/3 by the techniques described in the log section. If a value of K, less than 2/3V is desired for a given application, an external op amp would be required as shown in Figure 6. The ratio of the two resistors is approximately:

$$R1/R_G = (1/K - 1) \text{ where } K = \text{desired scale factor}$$

Figure 6. Method for Adjusting $K < 2/3V$

161

ANALOG DEVICES

Economy, Wideband Log/Antilog Amplifiers

MODELS 759N, 759P

FEATURES
Low-Cost, Complete Log/Antilog Amplifier
External Components Not Required;
  Internal Reference; Temperature Compensated
Small Size: 1.1" x 1.1" x 0.4"
Fast Response: 200kHz Bandwidth (I_{SIG} = 1µA)
6 Decades Current Operation — 1nA to 1mA
  1% max Error — 20nA to 200µA
  2% max Error — 10nA to 1mA
4 Decades Voltages Operation — 1mV to 10V
  1% max Error — 1mV to 2V
  2% max Error — 1mV to 10V

APPLICATIONS
Log Current or Voltage
Antilog Voltage
Data Compression or Expansion

GENERAL DESCRIPTION
Models 759N and 759P are low cost, fast response, dc
logarithmic amplifiers offering 1% conformance to ideal log
operation over four decades of current operation — 20nA to
200µA, as well as 2% conformance over four decades of voltage operation — 1mV to 10V. Featuring 200kHz bandwidth at
I_{SIG} = 1µA, these new economy designs are the industry's

suited for log applications whenever low cost implementation
of logarithmic natural relationships is advantages. Examples
are absorbence measurements, data compression and expansion, chemical analysis of liquids, computing powers, roots and
ratios and conversion of exponential quantities to linear form.

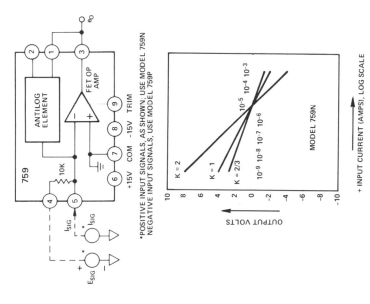

Figure 1. Functional Block Diagram and Transfer Function

fastest log/antilog amplifiers and offer an attractive alternative to in-house designs.

Designed for ease of use, models 759N/P are complete, temperature compensated, log or antilog amplifiers packaged in a small 1.1″ x 1.1″ x 0.4″ epoxy encapsulated module. External components are not required for logging currents over the complete six decade operating range from 1nA to 1mA. Both the scale factor (K = 2, 1, 2/3 volt/decade) and log/antilog operation can be selected by simple pin interconnection. In addition both the internal 10µA reference current as well as the offset voltage may be externally adjusted to improve overall accuracy performance.

MODEL SELECTION

Model 759N computes the log of positive input signals (voltage or current), while model 759P computes the log of negative input signals (voltage or current). In the antilog mode of operation, both models accept bipolar voltage input signals ($-2V \leqslant E_{SIG}/K \leqslant 2V$), with model 759N producing a positive output signal and model 759P producing a negative output signal.

APPLICATIONS

Model 759N and 759P can operate with either current or voltage inputs when connected as shown in Figure 1. To illustrate the logarithmic transfer characteristics, a plot of input current versus output voltage is also presented. Model 759 is ideally

P.O. Box 280; Norwood, Massachusetts 02062 U.S.A.
Telex: 924491 **Cables: ANALOG NORWOODMASS**

Information furnished by Analog Devices is believed to be accurate and reliable. However, no responsibility is assumed by Analog Devices for its use; nor for any infringements of patents or other rights of third parties which may result from its use. No license is granted by implication or otherwise under any patent or patent rights of Analog Devices.

SPECIFICATIONS (typical @ +25°C and V_S = ±15V dc unless otherwise noted)

MODEL	759N/P
TRANSFER FUNCTIONS	
Current Mode	$e_O = -K \log_{10} \dfrac{I_{SIG}}{I_{REF}}$
Voltage Mode	$e_O = -K \log_{10} \dfrac{E_{SIG}}{E_{REF}}$
Antilog Mode	$e_O = E_{REF} \, 10^{\left(\dfrac{E_{SIG}}{K}\right)}$
TRANSFER FUNCTION PARAMETERS	
Scale Factor (K) Selections[1],[2]	2, 1, 2/3 Volt/Decade
Error @ +25°C	±1% max
vs. Temperature (0 to +70°C)	±0.04%/°C max
Reference Voltage (E_{REF})[2]	0.1V
Error @ +25°C	±4% max
vs. Temperature (0 to +70°C)	±0.05%/°C
Reference Current (I_{REF})[2]	10μA
Error @ +25°C	±3% max
vs. Temperature (0 to +70°C)	±0.05%/°C

LOG CONFORMITY ERROR

I_{SIG} Range	E_{SIG} Range	R.T.I.	R.T.O. (K = 1)
20nA to 200μA	1mV to 2V	±1% max	±4.3mV max
10nA to 1mA	1mV to 10V	±2% max	±8.64mV max
1nA to 10nA		±5%	±21mV

INPUT SPECIFICATIONS

Current Signal Range	
Model 759N	+1nA to +1mA min
Model 759P	−1nA to −1mA min
Max Safe Input Current	±10mA max
Bias Current @ +25°C	(0, +) 200pA max
vs. Temperature (0 to +70°C)	x2/+10°C
Voltage Signal Range	
Model 759N	+1mV to +10V min
Model 759P	−1mV to −10V min
Offset Voltage @ +25°C (Adjustable to 0)	±2mV max
vs. Temperature (0 to +70°C)	±10μV/°C
vs. Supply Voltage	±15μV/%

OUTLINE DIMENSIONS
Dimensions shown in inches and (mm).

0.41 MAX (10.4)
0.04 DIA (1.02)
1.13 MAX (28.7)
0.2 TO 0.25 (5 TO 6.4)
1.13 MAX (28.7)

9 — TRIM
8 — −15
7 — COM
6 — +15
5 — I_{SIG}
4 — E_{SIG}
3 — e_{OUT}
2 — 2V/DEC
1 — 1V/DEC

100k
[1] OPTIONAL TRIM

BOTTOM VIEW

0.1 GRID (2.5)

WEIGHT: 10 GRAMS
MATING SOCKET AC1016 $5.00 (1—9)

[1] Optional 100kΩ external trim pot. Input offset voltage may be adjusted to zero with trim pot connected as shown. With trim terminal 9 left open, input offset voltage will be ±2mV maximum.

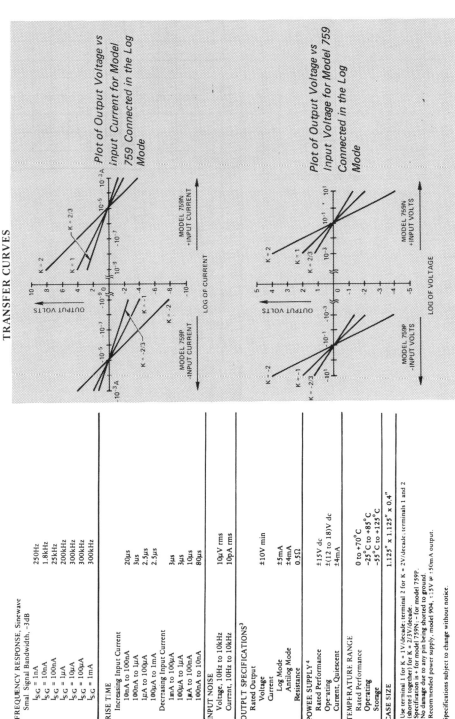

TRANSFER CURVES

Plot of Output Voltage vs Input Current for Model 759 Connected in the Log Mode

Plot of Output Voltage vs Input Voltage for Model 759 Connected in the Log Mode

---

FREQUENCY RESPONSE, Sinewave

Small Signal Bandwidth, −3dB

$I_{SG} = 1nA$	250Hz
$I_{SG} = 10nA$	1.8kHz
$I_{SG} = 100nA$	25kHz
$I_{SG} = 1\mu A$	200kHz
$I_{SG} = 10\mu A$	300kHz
$I_{SG} = 100\mu A$	300kHz
$I_{SG} = 1mA$	300kHz

RISE TIME

Increasing Input Current

10nA to 100nA	20μs
100nA to 1μA	3μs
1μA to 100μA	2.5μs
100μA to 1mA	2.5μs

Decreasing Input Current

1mA to 100μA	3μs
100μA to 1μA	3μs
1μA to 100nA	10μs
100nA to 10nA	80μs

INPUT NOISE

Voltage, 10Hz to 10kHz	10μV rms
Current, 10Hz to 10kHz	10pA rms

OUTPUT SPECIFICATIONS[3]

Rated Output

Voltage	±10V min

Current

Log Mode	±5mA
Antilog Mode	±4mA
Resistance	0.5Ω

POWER SUPPLY[4]

Rated Performance	±15V dc
Operating	±(12 to 18)V dc
Current, Quiescent	±4mA

TEMPERATURE RANGE

Rated Performance	0 to +70°C
Operating	−25°C to +85°C
Storage	−55°C to +125°C

CASE SIZE	1.125" x 1.125" x 0.4"

[1] Use terminal 1 for K = 1V/decade; terminal 2 for K = 2V/decade; terminals 1 and 2 (shorted together) for K = 2/3V/decade.

[2] Specification is + for model 759N; − for model 759P.

[3] No damage due to any pin being shorted to ground.

[4] Recommended power supply, model 904, ±15V @ ±50mA output.

Specifications subject to change without notice.

Understanding the Log Amplifier Performance

PRINCIPLE OF OPERATION

Log operation is obtained by placing the antilog element in the feedback loop of the op amp as shown in Figure 1. At the summing junction, terminal 5, the input signal current to be processed is summed with the output current of the antilog element. To attain a balance of these two currents, the op amp provides the required output voltage to the antilog feedback element. Under these conditions the ideal transfer equation (K = 1) is:

$$e_{OUT} = 1V \log_{10} I_{SIG}/I_{REF}$$

The log is a mathematical operator which is defined only for numbers, which are dimensionless quantities. Since an input current would have the dimensions of amperes it must be referenced to another current, I_{REF}, the ratio being dimensionless. For this purpose a temperature compensated reference of $10\mu A$ is generated internally.

The scale factor, K, is a multiplying constant. For a change in input current of one decade (decade = ratio of 10:1), the output changes by K volts. K may be selected as 1V or 2V by connecting the output to pin 1 or 2, respectively. If the output is connected to both pins 1 and 2, K will be 2/3V.

REFERRING ERRORS TO INPUT

A unique property of log amplifiers is that a dc error of any given amount at the output corresponds to a constant percent of the input, regardless of input level. To illustrate this, consider the output effects due to changing the input by 1%.

SOURCES OF ERROR

Log Conformity Error – Log conformity in logarithmic devices is a specification similar to linearity in linear devices. Log conformity error is the difference between the value of the transfer equation and the actual value which occurs at the output of the log module, after scale factor, reference and offset errors are eliminated or taken into account. Figure 2 below illustrates the log conformity performance of model 759 over a 6 decade input range. The best linearity performance is obtained in the 5 decades from 10nA to 1mA. To obtain optimum performance, the input data should be scaled to this range.

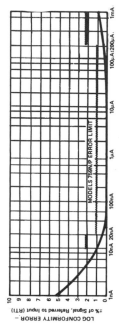

Figure 2. *Log Conformity Error for Models 759N and 759P*

Offset Voltage – The offset voltage, E_{os}, of model 759 is the offset voltage of the internal FET amplifier. This voltage appears as a small dc offset voltage in series with the input terminals. For current logging applications, its error contribution is negligible. However, for log voltage applications, best performance is obtained by an offset trim adjustment.

The output would be:

$$e_{OUT} = 1V \log_{10}(I_{SIG}/I_{REF})(1.01) \text{ which is equivalent to:}$$

$$e_{OUT} = \underbrace{1V \log_{10}(I_{SIG}/I_{REF})}_{Initial\ Value}, \underbrace{\pm 1V \log_{10}(1.01)}_{Change}$$

The change in output, due to a 1% input change is a constant value of ±4.3mV. Conversely, a dc error at the output of ±4.3mV is equivalent to a change at the input of 1%. An abbreviated table is presented below for converting between errors referred to output (R.T.O.), and errors referred to input (R.T.I.).

| | ERROR R.T.O. | | |
ERROR R.T.I.	K = 1	K = 2	K = 2/3
0.1%	0.43mV	0.86mV	0.28mV
0.5	2.17	4.34	1.45
1.0	4.32	8.64	2.88
3.0	12.84	25.68	8.56
4.0	17.03	34.06	11.35
5.0	21.19	42.38	14.13
10.0	41.39	82.78	27.59

Table 1. Converting Output Error in mV to Input Error in %

Bias Current – The bias current of model 759 is the bias current of the internal FET amplifier. This parameter can be a significant source of error when processing signals in the nanoamp region. For this reason, the bias current for model 759 is 200pA, maximum.

Reference Current – I_{REF} is the internally generated current source to which all input currents are compared. I_{REF} tolerance errors appear as a dc offset at the output. The specified value of I_{REF} is ±3% referred to the input, and, from Table 1, corresponds to a dc offset of ±12.84mV for K = 1. This offset is independent of input signal and may be removed by injecting a current into terminal 1 or 2.

Reference Voltage – E_{REF} is the effective internally generated voltage to which all input voltages are compared. It is related to I_{REF} through the equation:

$$E_{REF} = I_{REF} \times R_{IN}$$, where R_{IN} is an internal 10kΩ, precision resistor. Virtually all tolerance in E_{REF} is due to I_{REF}. Consequently, variations in I_{REF} cause a shift in E_{REF}.

Scale Factor – Scale factor is the voltage change at the output for a decade (i.e., 10:1) change at the input, when connected in the log mode. Error in scale factor is equivalent to a change in gain, or slope, and is specified in per cent of the nominal value. An external adjustment may be performed if fine trimming is desired for improved accuracy.

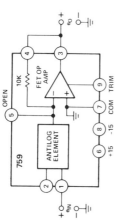

Figure 4. Functional Block Diagram

OPTIONAL EXTERNAL ADJUSTMENTS FOR LOG OPERATION

Trimming E_{OS} – The amplifier's offset voltage, E_{OS}, may be trimmed for improved accuracy with the model 759 connected in its log circuit. To accomplish this, a 100kΩ, 10 turn pot is connected as shown in Figure 3. The input terminal, Pin 4, is connected to ground. Under these conditions the output voltage is:

$$e_{OUT} = -K \log_{10} E_{OS}/E_{REF}$$

To obtain an offset voltage of 100µV or less, for K = 1, the trim pot should be adjusted until the output voltage is between +3 and +4 volts for model 759N, and –3 to –4V for model 759P.

For other values of K, the trim pot should be adjusted for an output of e_{OUT} = 3 x K to 4 x K where K is the scale factor.

Principle of Operation – The antilog element converts the voltage input, appearing at terminal 1 or 2, to a current which is proportional to the antilog of the applied voltage. The current-to-voltage conversion is then completed by the feedback resistor in a closed-loop op amp circuit.

A more complete expression for the antilog function is:

$$e_{OUT} = E_{REF} \, 10^{-e_{IN}/K} + E_{OS}$$

The terms K, E_{OS}, and E_{REF} are those described previously in the LOG section.

Offset Voltage (E_{OS}) Adjustment – Although offset voltage of the antilog circuit may be balanced by connecting it in the log mode, and using the technique described previously, it may be more advantageous to use the circuit of Figure 5. In this configuration, offset voltage is equal to $e_{OUT}/100$. Adjust for the desired null, using the 100k trim pot. After adjusting, turn power off, remove the external 100Ω resistor, and the jumper from Pin 1 to +15V. For 759P use the same procedure but connect Pin 1 to –15V.

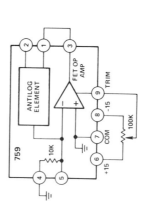

Figure 3. Trimming E_{OS} in Log Mode

Reference Current or Reference Voltage – The reference current or voltage of model 759 may be shifted by injecting a constant current into the unused scale factor terminal (Pin 1 or Pin 2). Each 330µA of current injected will shift the reference one decade, in accordance with the expression: $I_I = 330\mu A \log 10\mu A/I_{REF}$, where I_I = current to be injected and I_{REF} = the desired reference current.

By changing I_{REF}, there is a corresponding change in E_{REF} since, $E_{REF} = I_{REF} \times R_{IN}$. An alternate method for rescaling E_{REF} is to connect an external R_{IN}, at the I_{IN} terminal (Pin 5) to supplant the 10kΩ supplied internally (leaving it unconnected). The expression for E_{REF} is then, $E_{REF} = R_{IN} I_{REF}$. Care must be taken to choose R_{IN} such that $(e_{SIG}\ max)/R_{IN} \leqslant 1mA$.

Scale Factor (K) Adjustment – Scale factor may be increased from its nominal value by inserting a series resistor between the output terminal, Pin 3, and either terminal 1 or 2. The table below should be consulted when making these scale factor changes.

RANGE OF K	CONNECT SERIES R TO PIN	VALUE OF R	NOTE
2/3V to 1.01V	1	3kΩ x (K − 2/3)	use pins 1, 2
1.01V to 2.02V	1	3kΩ x (K − 1)	use pin 1
>2.02V	2	3kΩ x (K − 2)	use pin 2

Table 2. Resistor Selection Chart for Shifting Scale Factor

ANTILOG OPERATION

The model 759 may be used to develop the antilog of the input voltage when connected as shown in Figure 4. The antilog transfer function (an exponential), is:

$$e_{OUT} = E_{REF}\ 10^{-e_{IN}/K} \qquad [-2 \leqslant e_{IN}/K \leqslant 2]$$

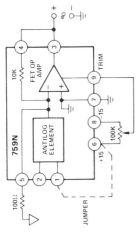

Figure 5. Trimming E_{OS} in Antilog Mode

Reference Voltage (E_{REF}) Adjustment – In antilog operation, the voltage reference appears as a multiplying constant. E_{REF} adjustment may be accomplished by connecting a resistor, R, from Pin 5 to Pin 3, in place of the internal 10kΩ. The value of R is determined by:

$$R = E_{REF}\ desired/10^{-5}\ A$$

Scale Factor (K) Adjustment – The scale factor may be adjusted for all values of K greater than 2/3V by the techniques described in the log section. If a value of K. less than 2/3V is desired for a given application, an external op amp would be required as shown in Figure 6. The ratio of the two resistors is approximately:

$$R1/R_G = (1/K - 1)\ \text{where K = desired scale factor}$$

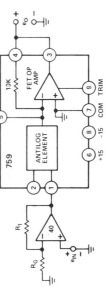

Figure 6. Method for Adjusting K<2/3V

169

4423

microcomputer peripherals/power supplies
signal conditioning components/amplifiers
data acquisition systems/data converters

microcomputer peripherals/power supplies
signal conditioning components/amplifiers
data acquisition systems/data converters
microcomputer peripherals/power supplies
signal conditioning components/amplifiers
data acquisition systems/data converters
microcomputer peripherals/power supplies
signal conditioning components/amplifiers

microcomputer peripherals/power supplies
signal conditioning components/amplifiers
data acquisition systems/data converters
microcomputer peripherals/power supplies
signal conditioning components/amplifiers
data acquisition systems/data converters
microcomputer peripherals/power supplies
signal conditioning components/amplifiers
data acquisition systems/data converters
microcomputer peripherals/power supplies
signal conditioning components/amplifiers

PRECISION
QUADRATURE OSCILLATOR

Sin $2\pi ft$

Cos $2\pi ft$

FEATURES

Sine and Cosine Outputs
Resistor Programmable Frequency
Wide Frequency Range
   0.002 Hz to 20 kHz
Low Distortion
   0.2% max up to 5 kHz
Easy Adjustments
Small Size
Low Cost

DESCRIPTION

The Model 4423 is a precision quadrature oscillator. It has two outputs 90 degrees out of phase with each other, thus providing sine and cosine wave outputs available at the same time. The 4423 is resistor programmable and is easy to use. It has low distortion (0.2% max up to 5 kHz) and excellent frequency and amplitude stability.

The Model 4423 also includes an uncommitted operational amplifier which may be used as a buffer, a level shifter or as an independent operational amplifier. The 4423 is packaged in a versatile, small, low cost DIP package.

171

SPECIFICATIONS

Prices and Specifications
subject to change without notice

Specifications typical at 25°C and ±15VDC
Power Supply Unless Otherwise Noted.

ELECTRICAL

	MIN	TYP	MAX	UNITS
FREQUENCY				
Initial Frequency (no adjustments)	20.0k	20.5	21.0k	Hz
Frequency Range (using 2 R's only)	2k		20k	Hz
Frequency Range (using 2 R's and 2 C's)	.0002		20k	Hz
Accuracy of Frequency Equation*		±1	±5	%
Stability vs Temperature		±50	±100	ppm/°C
Quadrature Phase Error		±0.1		degree
DISTORTION				
Sine Output (pin 1)				
0.002Hz to 5kHz			0.2	%
5kHz to 20kHz			0.5	%
Cosine Output (pin 7)				
0.002Hz to 5kHz		0.2		%
5kHz to 20kHz		0.8		%
Distortion vs Temperature		0.015		%/°C
OUTPUT				
Amplitude (Sine)				
At 20 kHz	6.5	7	7.5	V rms
vs Temperature		0.05		%/°C
vs Supply		0.4		V/V
Output Current	1.5	5		mA
Output impedance			1	Ω

MECHANICAL

12.7mm (0.50")
6.4mm (0.25")
20.3mm (0.80")
0.51mm (0.020")
4.6mm (0.18")
Pin 14
Pin 1
Dot over Pin 1

ROW SPACING - 7.6 (0.300")
WEIGHT - 3.4 gms (0.12 oz)
CONNECTOR - 14 pin DIP connector

Pin material and plating composition
conform to method 2003 (solderability)
of MIL-STD-883 (except paragraph 3.2).

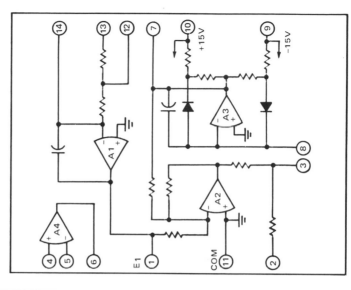

FIGURE 1. Equivalent Circuit.

UNCOMMITTED OP AMP

Input Offset Voltage			1.5	mV
Input Bias Current			275	nA
Input Impedance			1	MΩ
Open Loop Gain			90	dB
Output Current		5		mA

POWER SUPPLY

Rated Supply Voltage		±12	±15	VDC
Supply Voltage Range			±18	VDC
Quiescent Current			±9 / ±18	mA

TEMPERATURE RANGE

Specifications	0	+70	°C
Operation	-25	+85	°C
Storage	-55	+125	°C

* May be trimmed for better accuracy.

PIN CONNECTIONS

1. E_1, Sine Output
2. Frequency Adjustment
3. Frequency Adjustment
4. +In, Uncommitted Op Amp
5. -In, Uncommitted Op Amp
6. Output, Uncommitted Op Amp
7. E_2, Cosine Output
8. Frequency Adjustment
9. $-V_{cc}$, -15VDC
10. $+V_{cc}$, +15VDC
11. Common
12. Frequency Adjustment
13. Frequency Adjustment
14. Frequency Adjustment

TYPICAL PERFORMANCE CURVES

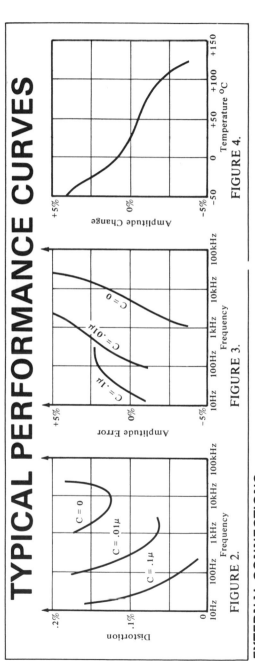

FIGURE 2.

FIGURE 3.

FIGURE 4.

FIGURE 7.

For best results, the capacitor values shown in Table I should be selected with respect to their frequency ranges.

EXTERNAL CONNECTIONS

I. 20 kHz Quadrature Oscillator

The 4423 does not require any external component to obtain a 20 kHz quadrature oscillator. The connection diagram is as shown in Figure 5.

FIGURE 5.

2. Resistor Programmable Quadrature Oscillator

For resistor programmable frequencies in the 2 kHz to

f	20 kHz to 2 kHz	2 kHz to 200 Hz	200 Hz to 20 Hz
C	0	0.01µF	0.1µF
20 Hz to 2 Hz	2 Hz to 0.2 Hz	0.2 Hz to 0.02 Hz	0.02 Hz to 0.002 Hz
1µF	10µF	100µF	1000µF

TABLE I.

After selecting the capacitor for a particular frequency the value of the required resistor can be obtained by using the resistor selection curve shown in Figure 8 or by the expression:

$$R = \frac{3.785f\,(C + 0.001)}{42.05 - 2f\,(C + 0.001)}$$

where,
R is in kΩ
f is in Hz
and C is in µF

20 kHz frequency range, the connection diagram is shown in Figure 6. Note that only two resistors of equal value are required. The resistor R can be expressed by,

$$R = \frac{3.785f}{42.05 - 2f}$$, R in kΩ
f in kHz

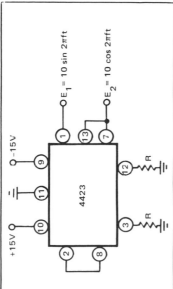

$E_1 = 10 \sin 2\pi f t$

$E_2 = 10 \cos 2\pi f t$

FIGURE 6.

3. Quadrature Oscillator Programmable to 0.002 Hz

For oscillator frequencies below 2000 Hz, use of two capacitors of equal value and two resistors of equal value as shown in Figure 7 is recommended. Connections shown in Figure 7 can be used to get oscillator frequency in the 0.002 Hz to 20 kHz range.

The frequency f can be expressed by:

$$f = \frac{42.05\,R}{(C + 0.001)\,(3.785 + 2R)}$$

where, f is in Hz
C is in µF
and R is in kΩ

DISSIPATION FACTOR (DF)

A capacitor can be modeled by an ideal capacitor in parallel with an internal resistor whose value depends on its dissipation factor (DF). Mathematically, the internal resistor R is given by,

$$R = \frac{1}{2\pi f \, C(DF)}$$

where R is in Ω, f is the Hz, and C is in farads.

For example, the DF of ceramic disc capacitors is of the order of 3%, which for a 0.01 μF capacitor would look like having an internal resistor of 530kΩ at 1 kHz. The 530 kΩ value resistor is small enough to stop the 4423 oscillator from oscillating.

Some capacitor manufacturers use the terms "Power Factor" (PF) or "Q Factor" (Q) instead of the term "Dissipation Factor". These terms are similar in meaning and are mathematically related by,

$$(PF) = \frac{(DF)}{\sqrt{1 + (DF)^2}} \quad ; \quad Q = \frac{1}{(DF)}$$

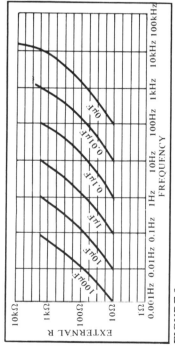

FIGURE 8.

The curves shown in Figure 8 are provided only as a nomographic design aid. The selection of capacitor values is not limited to the values shown in Figure 8. Any suitable combination of R and C values which satisfies the expression relating R, F and C as shown above, would work satisfactorily with the 4423.

NOTES ON TYPES OF CAPACITORS TO USE:

There are various kinds of capacitors available for use. There are polarized, also known as DC capacitors and non-polarized, also known as AC capacitors available. Of these two types, the polarized capacitors cannot be used with 4423 to set the frequencies.

Commonly available non-polarized capacitors include NPO ceramic, silver mica, teflon, polystyrene, polycarbonate, mylar, ceramic disc etc. A comparison is shown in Table II.

OSCILLATION AMPLITUDE

It takes a finite time to build up the amplitude of the oscillation to its final full scale value. There is a relationship between the amplitude build-up time and the frequency. The lower the frequency, the longer the amplitude build-up time. For example, typically it takes 250 seconds at 1 Hz, 30 seconds at 10 Hz, 4 seconds at 100 Hz, 400 milliseconds at 1 kHz, and 40 milliseconds at 10 kHz oscillator frequencies.

There are two methods available to shorten this normal amplitude build-up time. But there is also a relationship between the amplitude build-up time and distortion at final amplitude value. When the amplitude build-up time is shortened, the distortion can get worse.

One method to shorten the amplitude build-up time is to connect a resistor between pin 3 and pin 14. The lower this resistor is the shorter will be the time to build up amplitude of the oscillation, and worse will be the distortion of the output waveform. For example, a 100kΩ resistor would shorten the amplitude build up time from 15 seconds to 1 second at 20 Hz frequency, but the distortion could be degraded from typically 0.05% to 0.5%.

The other method is to momentarily insert a 1kΩ resistor via a reset switch betwen pin 3 and pin 14. The amplitude of oscillation is built up instantaneously when the reset switch is pushed. There will be no degradation of distortion with this method since the 1kΩ resistor does not remain in the circuit continuously.

	Capacitance Range (µF)	Temperature Coefficients ppm/°C	Dissipation Factor (%)
NPO Ceramic	5pF - 0.1 µF	30	0.05
Silver Mica	5pF - 0.047 µF	60	0.05
Teflon	0.001 - 100 µF	200	0.01
Polystyrene	0.001 - 500 µF	100	0.03
Polycarbonate	0.001 - 1000 µF	90	0.08
Metalized Teflon	0.001 - 100 µF	60	0.1
Metalized Polycarbonate	0.001 - 1000 µF	10	0.4
Mylar	0.001 - 1000 µF	700	0.7
Metalized Mylar	0.001 - 2000 µF	700	1
Ceramic Disc	5pF - 0.5 µF	10,000	3

TABLE II.

For use with the 4423 oscillator, the choice of capacitors depends mainly on the user's application, error budget and cost budget. Note that the specifications of 4423 do not include the error contribution of the external components. The errors sourced by external components normally have to be added to the 4423 specifications.

As a general selection criteria we recommend the use of the above table. Start from the top of the list in the above table. If the capacitor is found unsuitable due to it being too large in size, too expensive, or is not easily available, then move down in the list for the next best selection. In any case do not choose or use any capacitors with dissipation factors greater than 1%. Such a capacitor would stop 4423 oscillation.

LF353B-1 / LF353A / LF353B / LF353
Wide Bandwidth Dual JFET Input Operational Amplifiers

FEBRUARY 1980

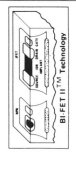

BI-FET II™ Technology

National Semiconductor

LF353 Wide Bandwidth Dual JFET Input Operational Amplifiers

General Description

These devices are low cost, high speed, dual JFET input operational amplifiers with an internally trimmed input offset voltage (BI-FET II™ technology). They require low supply current yet maintain a large gain bandwidth product and fast slew rate. In addition, well matched high voltage JFET input devices provide very low input bias and offset currents. The LF353 is pin compatible with the standard LM1558 allowing designers to immediately upgrade the overall performance of existing LM1558 and LM358 designs.

These amplifiers may be used in applications such as high speed integrators, fast D/A converters, sample and hold circuits and many other circuits requiring low input offset voltage, low input bias current, high input impedance, high slew rate and wide bandwidth. The devices also exhibit low noise and offset voltage drift.

Features

■ Internally trimmed offset voltage 2 mV
■ Low input bias current 50 pA
■ Low input noise voltage 16 nV/$\sqrt{\text{Hz}}$
■ Low input noise current 0.01 pA/$\sqrt{\text{Hz}}$
■ Wide gain bandwidth 4 MHz
■ High slew rate 13 V/μs
■ Low supply current 3.6 mA
■ High input impedance $10^{12}\Omega$
■ Low total harmonic distortion $A_V = 10$, $R_L = 10k$, $V_O = 20\,Vp-p$, BW = 20 Hz-20 kHz <0.02%
■ Low 1/f noise corner 50 Hz
■ Fast settling time to 0.01% 2 μs

Connection Diagrams

Typical Connection

LF353H Metal Can Package (Top View)

OUTPUT A
INVERTING INPUT A
NON-INVERTING INPUT A
OUTPUT B
INVERTING INPUT B
NON-INVERTING INPUT B

Order Number LF353AH or LF353BH
See NS Package H08C

LF353N Dual-In-Line Package (Top View)

OUTPUT A
INVERTING INPUT A
NON-INVERTING INPUT A
V⁻
V⁺
OUTPUT B
INVERTING INPUT B
NON-INVERTING INPUT B

Order Number LF353AN, LF353BN or LF353N
See NS Package N08A

Simplified Schematic

1/2 Dual

INTERNALLY TRIMMED
INTERNALLY TRIMMED

1980 National Semiconductor Corp.

DA-FL25M20/Printed in U.S.A.

Absolute Maximum Ratings

Supply Voltage	±18V
Power Dissipation (Note 1)	500mW
Operating Temperature Range	0°C to +70°C
$T_{j(MAX)}$	115°C
Differential Input Voltage	±30V
Input Voltage Range (Note 2)	±15V
Output Short Circuit Duration	Continuous
Storage Temperature Range	−65°C to +150°C
Lead Temperature (Soldering, 10 seconds)	300°C

DC Electrical Characteristics (Note 4)

SYMBOL	PARAMETER	CONDITIONS	LF353A			LF353B and LF353B-1			LF353			UNITS
			MIN	TYP	MAX	MIN	TYP	MAX	MIN	TYP	MAX	
V_{OS}	Input Offset Voltage	$R_S = 10k\Omega$, $T_A = 25°C$		1	2		3	5		5	10	mV
		Over Temperature			4			7			13	mV
$\Delta V_{OS}/\Delta T$	Average TC of Input Offset Voltage LF351B-1	$R_S = 10k\Omega$		10			10			10		$\mu V/°C$
												$\mu V/°C$
I_{OS}	Input Offset Current	$T_j = 25°C$, (Notes 4, 5)		25	100		25	100		25	100	pA
		$T_j \leqslant 70°C$			2			4			4	nA
I_B	Input Bias Current	$T_j = 25°C$, (Notes 4, 5)		50	200		50	200		50	200	pA
		$T_j \leqslant 70°C$			4			8			8	nA
R_{IN}	Input Resistance	$T_j = 25°C$		10^{12}			10^{12}			10^{12}		Ω
A_{VOL}	Large Signal Voltage Gain	$V_S = \pm15V$, $T_A = 25°C$, $V_O = \pm10V$, $R_L = 2k\Omega$	50	100		50	100		25	100		V/mV
		Over Temperature	25			25			15			V/mV
V_O	Output Voltage Swing	$V_S = \pm15V$, $R_L = 10k\Omega$	±12	±13.5		±12	±13.5		±12	±13.5		V
V_{CM}	Input Common-Mode Voltage Range	$V_S = \pm15V$	±11	+15		±11	+15		±11	+15		V
				−12			−12			−12		V
CMRR	Common-Mode Rejection Ratio	$R_S \leqslant 10k\Omega$	80	100		80	100		70	100		dB
PSRR	Supply Voltage Rejection Ratio	(Note 6)	90	100		80	100		70	100		dB
I_S	Supply Current			3.6	5.6		3.6	5.6		3.6	6.5	mA

AC Electrical Characteristics (Note 4)

SYMBOL	PARAMETER	CONDITIONS	LF353A			LF353B			LF353			UNITS
			MIN	TYP	MAX	MIN	TYP	MAX	MIN	TYP	MAX	
	Amplifier to Amplifier Coupling	$T_A = 25°C$, $f = 1$Hz–20kHz (Input Referred)		−120			−120			−120		dB
SR	Slew Rate	$V_S = ±15V$, $T_A = 25°C$		13			13			13		V/µs
GBW	Gain Bandwidth Product	$V_S = ±15V$, $T_A = 25°C$		4			4			4		MHz
e_n	Equivalent Input Noise Voltage	$T_A = 25°C$, $R_S = 100Ω$, $f = 1000$Hz		16			16			16		nV/√Hz
i_n	Equivalent Input Noise Current	$T_j = 25°C$, $f = 1000$Hz		0.01			0.01			0.01		pA/√Hz

Note 1: For operating at elevated temperature, the device must be derated based on a thermal resistance of 160°C/W junction to ambient for the N package, and 150°C/W junction to ambient for the H package.

Note 2: Unless otherwise specified the absolute maximum negative input voltage is equal to the negative power supply voltage.

Note 3: The power dissipation limit, however, cannot be exceeded.

Note 4: These specifications apply for $V_S = ±15V$ and $0°C ≤ T_A ≤ +70°C$. V_{OS}, I_B and I_{OS} are measured at $V_{CM} = 0$.

Note 5: The input bias currents are junction leakage currents which approximately double for every 10°C increase in the junction temperature, T_j. Due to the limited production test time, the input bias currents measured are correlated to junction temperature. In normal operation the junction temperature rises above the ambient temperature as a result of internal power dissipation, P_D. $T_j = T_A + θ_{jA} P_D$ where $θ_{jA}$ is the thermal resistance from junction to ambient. Use of a heat sink is recommended if input bias current is to be kept to a minimum.

Note 6: Supply voltage rejection ratio is measured for both supply magnitudes increasing or decreasing simultaneously in accordance with common practice.

181

Typical Performance Characteristics

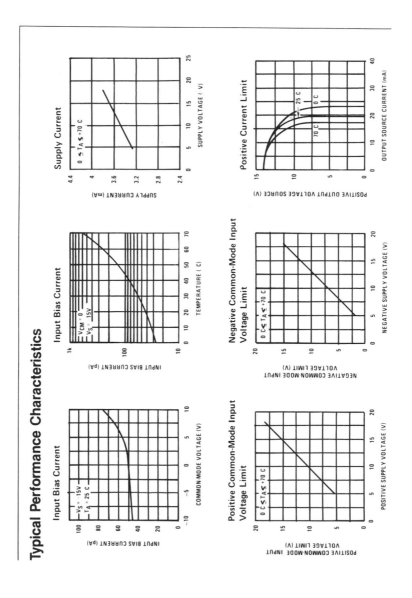

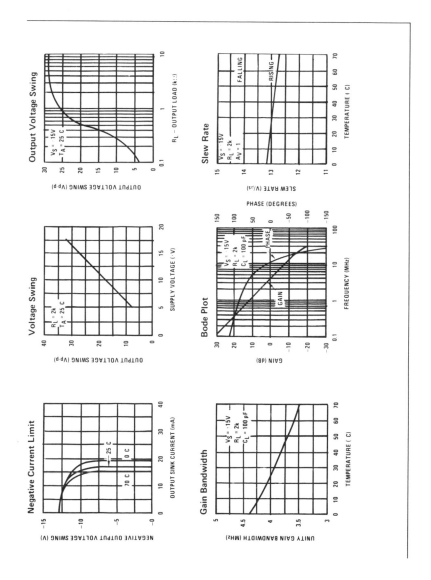

Output Voltage Swing

OUTPUT VOLTAGE SWING (Vp-p)

$V_S = 15V$
$T_A = 25\ C$

R_L — OUTPUT LOAD (kΩ)

Slew Rate

SLEW RATE (V/μs)

$V_S = 15V$
$R_L = 2k$
$A_V = 1$

FALLING

RISING

TEMPERATURE (C)

PHASE (DEGREES)

Voltage Swing

OUTPUT VOLTAGE SWING (Vp-p)

$R_L = 2k$
$T_A = 25\ C$

SUPPLY VOLTAGE (±V)

Bode Plot

GAIN (dB)

$V_S = 15V$
$R_L = 2k$
$C_L = 100\ pF$

PHASE

GAIN

FREQUENCY (MHz)

Negative Current Limit

NEGATIVE OUTPUT VOLTAGE SWING (V)

25 C

0 C

70 C

OUTPUT SINK CURRENT (mA)

Gain Bandwidth

UNITY GAIN BANDWIDTH (MHz)

$V_S = 15V$
$R_L = 2k$
$C_L = 100\ pF$

TEMPERATURE (C)

Typical Performance Characteristics (Continued)

Undistorted Output Voltage Swing

Open Loop Frequency Response

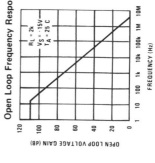

Distortion vs Frequency

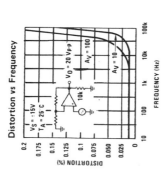

Common-Mode Rejection Ratio

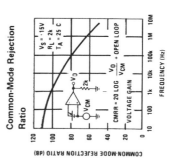

Equivalent Input Noise Voltage

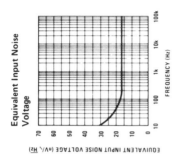

Power Supply Rejection Ratio

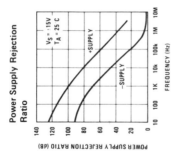

Inverter Settling Time

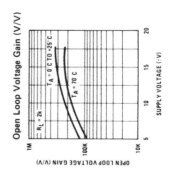

Output Impedance

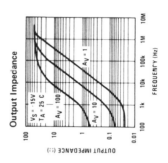

Open Loop Voltage Gain (V/V)

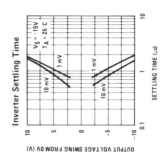

Pulse Response

Small Signal Inverting

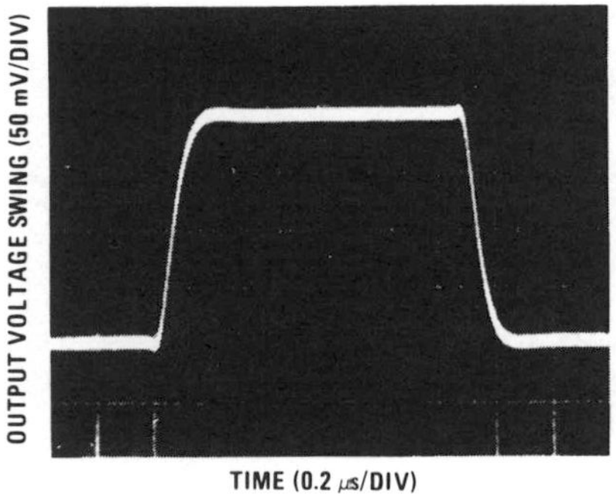

OUTPUT VOLTAGE SWING (50 mV/DIV)

TIME (0.2 µs/DIV)

Small Signal Non-Inverting

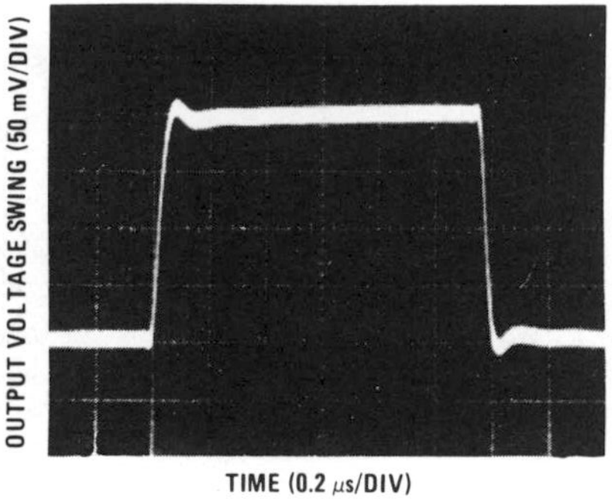

OUTPUT VOLTAGE SWING (50 mV/DIV)

TIME (0.2 µs/DIV)

Large Signal Inverting

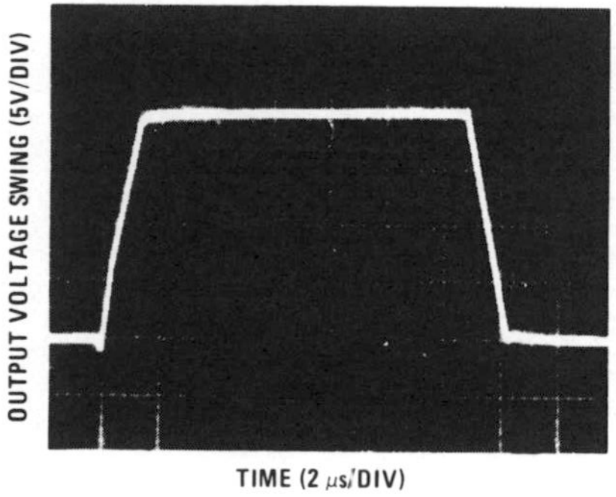

OUTPUT VOLTAGE SWING (5V/DIV)

TIME (2 µs/DIV)

Large Signal Non-Inverting

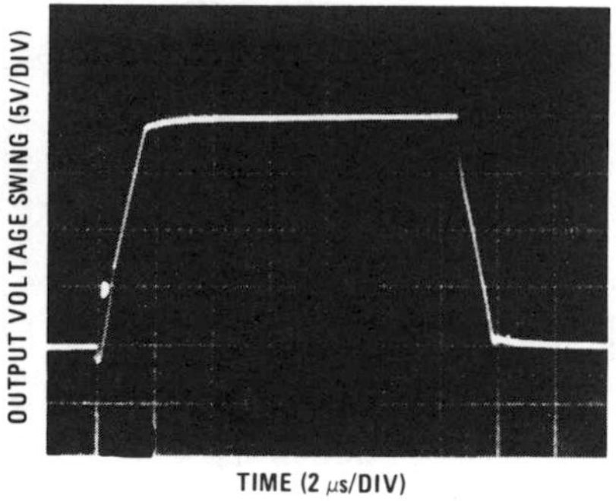

OUTPUT VOLTAGE SWING (5V/DIV)

TIME (2 µs/DIV)

186

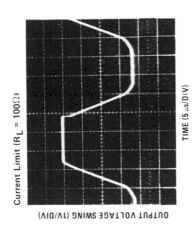

Current Limit (R_L = 100Ω)

OUTPUT VOLTAGE SWING (1V/DIV)

TIME (5 μs/DIV)

Application Hints

These devices are op amps with an internally trimmed input offset voltage and JFET input devices (BI-FET II). These JFETs have large reverse breakdown voltages from gate to source and drain eliminating the need for clamps across the inputs. Therefore, large differential input voltages can easily be accommodated without a large increase in input current. The maximum differential input voltage is independent of the supply voltages. However, neither of the input voltages should be allowed to exceed the negative supply as this will cause large currents to flow which can result in a destroyed unit.

Exceeding the negative common-mode limit on either input will cause a reversal of the phase to the output and force the amplifier output to the corresponding high or low state. Exceeding the negative common-mode limit on both inputs will force the amplifier output to a

187

Application Hints (Continued)

high state. In neither case does a latch occur since raising the input back within the common-mode range again puts the input stage and thus the amplifier in a normal operating mode.

Exceeding the positive common-mode limit on a single input will not change the phase of the output; however, if both inputs exceed the limit, the output of the amplifier will be forced to a high state.

The amplifiers will operate with a common-mode input voltage equal to the positive supply; however, the gain bandwidth and slew rate may be decreased in this condition. When the negative common-mode voltage swings to within 3V of the negative supply, an increase in input offset voltage may occur.

Each amplifier is individually biased by a zener reference which allows normal circuit operation on ±4V power supplies. Supply voltages less than these may result in lower gain bandwidth and slew rate.

The amplifiers will drive a 2 kΩ load resistance to ±10V over the full temperature range of 0°C to +70°C. If the amplifier is forced to drive heavier load currents, however, an increase in input offset voltage may occur on the negative voltage swing and finally reach an active current limit on both positive and negative swings.

Precautions should be taken to ensure that the power supply for the integrated circuit never becomes reversed in polarity or that the unit is not inadvertently installed backwards in a socket as an unlimited current surge through the resulting forward diode within the IC could cause fusing of the internal conductors and result in a destroyed unit.

Because these amplifiers are JFET rather than MOSFET input op amps they do not require special handling.

As with most amplifiers, care should be taken with lead dress, component placement and supply decoupling in order to ensure stability. For example, resistors from the output to an input should be placed with the body close to the input to minimize "pick-up" and maximize the frequency of the feedback pole by minimizing the capacitance from the input to ground.

A feedback pole is created when the feedback around any amplifier is resistive. The parallel resistance and capacitance from the input of the device (usually the inverting input) to AC ground set the frequency of the pole. In many instances the frequency of this pole is much greater than the expected 3 dB frequency of the closed loop gain and consequently there is negligible effect on stability margin. However, if the feedback pole is less than approximately 6 times the expected 3 dB frequency a lead capacitor should be placed from the output to the input of the op amp. The value of the added capacitor should be such that the RC time constant of this capacitor and the resistance it parallels is greater than or equal to the original feedback pole time constant.

Typical Application

Improved CMRR Instrumentation Amplifier

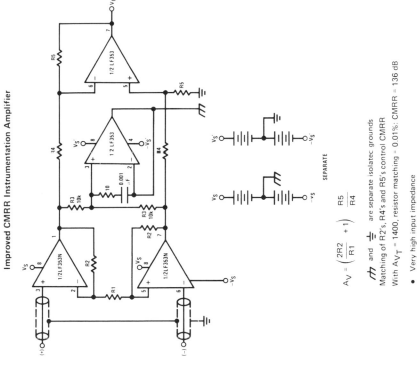

$$A_V = \left(\frac{2R2}{R1} + 1 \right) \frac{R5}{R4}$$

 and $\perp$ are separate isolatec grounds

Matching of R2's, R4's and R5's control CMRR

With A_{V_T} = 1400, resistor matching = 0.01%: CMRR = 136 dB

- Very high input impedance
- Super high CMRR

189

Bibliography

This Bibliography is divided into four sections. The four sections are: I. Operational Amplifiers and Computational Circuits; II. Linear and Nonlinear Differential Equations; III. Electronic Analog Computer Programming; IV. Process Measurement and Control.

I. Operational Amplifiers and Computational Circuits

Jung, W. G. 1980. *IC Op-Amp Cookbook*. Indianapolis: Howard W. Sams and Company, Inc.

Jacob, J. M. 1982. *Applications and Design with Analog Integrated Circuits*. Reston: Reston Publishing Company, Inc.

Stout, D. F. and Kaufman, M. 1976. *Handbook of Operational Amplifier Circuit Design*. New York: McGraw-Hill.

Graeme, J. G. Tobey, G. E. and Huelsman, L. P. 1971. *Operational Amplifiers*. New York: McGraw-Hill.

Irvine, R. G. 1981. *Operational Amplifier Characteristics and Applications.* Englewood Cliffs: Prentice-Hall, Inc.

Smith, J. I. 1971. *Modern Operational Circuit Design.* New York: Wiley-Interscience.

Korn, G. A. and Korn, T. M. 1964. *Electronic Analog and Hybrid Computers.* New York: McGraw-Hill.

Fox, H. W. 1978. *Master Op-Amp Applications Handbook.* Blue Ridge Summit: TAB BOOKS Inc.

Carr, J. J. 1983. *Linear IC/Op Amp Handbook.* Blue Ridge Summit: TAB BOOKS Inc.

Horn, D. T. 1984. *How to Design Op Amp Circuits, with Projects and Experiments.* Blue Ridge Summit: TAB BOOKS Inc.

II. Linear and Nonlinear Differential Equations

Boyce, W. E. and DiPrima, R. C. 1970. *Introduction to Differential Equations.* New York: John Wiley and Sons, Inc.

Davis, H. T. 1962. *Introduction to Nonlinear Differential and Integral Equations.* New York: Dover Publishing Company.

Arfken, G. 1970. *Mathematical Methods for Physicists.* New York: Academic Press.

Kreyszig, E. 1972. *Advanced Engineering Mathematics.* New York: John Wiley and Sons, Inc.

Butkov, E. 1968. *Mathematical Physics.* Reading: Addison-Wesley.

Sokolnikoff, I. S. and Redheffer, R. M. 1958. *Mathematics of Physics and Modern Engineering.* New York: McGraw-Hill.

Hagedorn, P. 1981. *Non-Linear Oscillations.* Oxford: Oxford University Press.

III. Electronic Analog Computer Programming

James, M. L., Smith, G. M. and Wolford, J. C. 1966. *Analog-Computer Simulation of En-*

gineering *Systems*. Scranton: International Textbook Company.

Rogers, A. E. and Connolly, T. W. 1960. *Analog Computation in Engineering Design*. New York: McGraw-Hill.

Franks, R. G. E. 1967. *Mathematical Modeling in Chemical Engineering*. New York: John Wiley and Sons, Inc.

Korn, G. A. and Korn, T. M. 1964. *Electronic Analog and Hybrid Computers*. New York: McGraw-Hill.

Karplus, W. J. 1958. *Analog Simulation*. New York: McGraw-Hill.

Jackson, A. S. 1960. *Analog Computation*. New York: McGraw-Hill.

Johnson, C. L. 1963. *Analog Computer Techniques*. New York: McGraw-Hill.

IV. Process Measurement and Control

Tedeschi, F. P. 1981. *How to Design, Build and Use Electronic Control Systems*. Blue Ridge Summit: TAB BOOKS Inc.

Kuecken, J. A. 1981. *How to Measure Anything with Electronic Instruments*. Blue Ridge Summit: TAB BOOKS Inc.

Coughanowr, D. R. and Koppel, L. B. 1965. *Process Systems Analysis and Control*. New York: McGraw-Hill.

Index

Index

pin connections for, 173
recommended capacitors for, 176
schematic for, 75
schematic for Burr-Brown 4423,
77
specifications for, 170-177
typical performance curve of, 174
quarter-square multiplication, 38

R

reference current, 159, 161, 167,
168
reference voltage, 160, 161, 167,
168
reference voltage source, 19
component layout for, 22
equation for, 20
front and rear view of, 22
schematic for, 20, 21
relay power supply, 16
layout for, 18
schematic for, 17

S

scale factor, 160, 161, 167, 169
second-order differential equations,
87
output from, 90
solution for, 89, 93
time-scaled solution for, 91
set point temperature, 107
simulation, 2
simultaneous differential equations,
94
solution for, 98
sine functions, generation of, 74
sinusoidal variation, 117, 121
square root IC, specifications for,
146-149
square roots, 35, 41, 42
IC multiplier, 46
trim procedures for, 151
squares, 35, 41
IC multiplier, 45
trim procedures for, 151
voltage, 41
steam pressure control, 137
proportional-integral control of,
139
proportional-integral-derivative
control of, 140
steam temperature control, 127
subtraction, 29
summing amplifier
construction hints for, 10
schematic for, 30

schematic symbol for, 9

T

temperature and rate of change of
temperature rate, 103
three-terminal voltage regulators, 15
time lag, 117
one-half cycle, 119
time scaling, 84
time vs. temperature control applications, 125, 126
transient response, 113
trim procedures, 43

U

uncontrolled system
effect of upset on, 108
model for, 106
temperature vs. time for, 107

V

Van der Pol's equation, 91, 94
schematic for, 95
solution plots for, 96
variable and slope chart (Fig. 9-16),
121
variable resistance method, 132
variable transconductance multiplication, 39
voltage, squaring, 41
variable transconductance multiplication, 36
volumetric flow rate, calculation for,
141

W

Wheatstone bridge, 132
wideband log/antilog amplifiers
antilog operation of, 169
applications for, 163
bias current in, 167
block diagram for, 163
functional block diagram for, 163
log conformity error in, 166
offset voltage in, 168
operational principle of, 166, 168
optional external adjustments for,
168
reference current in, 167, 168
reference voltage in, 167, 168
referring errors to input in, 166
scale factor adjustment in, 167,
169
sources of error in, 166
specifications for, 162-169
trimming in log mode of, 168

200

Edited by Roland S. Phelps